Do Great Things is fantastic! It challenges, encourages, and motivates. Few books connect the business world and the spiritual. Aaron Broyles shows how important that connection really is, and he does it in a compelling way. If you want to be all you can be—all you need to be—this book must be read!

DR. DOUG MUNTON, PASTOR OF FIRST BAPTIST CHURCH OF O'FALLON, ILLINOIS; AUTHOR OF *SEVEN STEPS TO BECOMING A HEALTHY CHRISTIAN LEADER*

How appropriate that a book titled *Do Great Things* would be authored by someone who has done and continues to do great things. How refreshing! I highly recommend reading this book!

TOM HOLLOWAY, PRESIDENT AND CEO, THE BANK OF EDWARDSVILLE

This is a great book for people who want to unlock the potential that is within their lives. It will help you think differently about yourself and uncover the unrealized opportunities that are before you, as you set out to launch in a new direction for your life. This can lead to the beginning of really doing great things for yourself and for others.

DR. LARRY RICHMOND, PH.D. IN EDUCATIONAL LEADERSHIP

Do Great Things empowers everyone in today's hectic world to sort through the competing priorities and demands on their lives based upon what they envision and choose to achieve. By maintaining a focus on character, family, community and faith, Aaron provides a roadmap for distilling the overload of information and options into a plan that inspires and motivates anyone toward success, from a practical application approach.

ROBERTS HUNTER, CEO, INFLIGHT PRODUCTIONS LTD.

William Carey said "Attempt great things for God; Expect great things from God." Aaron Broyles shows us how. He stands in that tradition of Christians who have reminded us that we need to dream big dreams. You will be inspired.

JOSH HUNT, AUTHOR OF *YOU CAN DOUBLE YOUR CLASS IN TWO YEARS OR LESS* AND *GOOD QUESTIONS HAVE GROUPS TALKING*

Do Great Things provides a values-based approach and practical tools to see opportunities and overcome obstacles, to help you achieve your potential.

BYRON BLACK, CAPTAIN, US COAST GUARD

Do you want to discover how to unlock the potential of your uniqueness and purpose in life, identify and prioritize what's really important, and gain the ability to see and develop opportunities that others do not see? If so, then I highly recommend you read this outstanding work, *Do Great Things*.

RICHARD KEMPER, EXECUTIVE DIRECTOR,
VIRGINIA INDEPENDENT SCHOOLS ATHLETIC ASSOCIATION

Do Great Things

Aaron Broyles

DO GREAT THINGS

Applying Proven Entrepreneurial Methods to Achieve Success in Everyday Life

Do Great Things:
Applying Proven Entrepreneurial Methods to Achieve Success in Everyday Life
© 2012 Aaron Broyles

Published by
Deep River Books•Sisters, Oregon
www.deepriverbooks.com

ISBN-13: 9781937756505
ISBN-10: 1937756505
Library of Congress: 2012943738

Printed in the United States of America

Cover design by David Litwin, Pure Fusion Media
Cover image: Rebecca Doehring

Some creative elements of this book designed by Justen Hong of Visual Lure

ACKNOWLEDGMENTS

·

I would like to thank my wife, Angie, who is my best friend and soul mate. I have learned more from her than anyone I know, and she has been an amazing encourager and inspiration throughout this entire ten-year process. This book would not exist were it not for her, and I am forever grateful. Angie, I will always love you.

I would also like to encourage each of my children, Wyatt, Will, Peyton, and Brooke, to live with purpose and do great things. You are each absolutely amazing just as God made you to be, and I am proud and blessed to be your father.

I am also so thankful and grateful for my father and mother, Bill and Sheri, for their encouragement and unconditional love. I am blessed beyond belief to be your son. I am equally grateful for my mother-in-law, Nancy, who is one of my greatest supporters, and I owe a great deal to my father-in-law, Larry, who has passed. I learned so much from him, and I miss him immensely.

Thank you to Rob Hunter for your insights, honest feedback, and ongoing encouragement. I consider you a great friend who never fails to tell me like it is.

I would like to thank Larry Richmond for everything he did in his support of this book and for his feedback. I am grateful for the opportunities he provided in the development and presentation of this material. Thank you for all the great brainstorming sessions, and thank you for being such a great friend.

I would like to acknowledge Doug Munton for his support, advice, and feedback. Doug has been a mentor, adviser, and most importantly, a great friend.

Thank you to Bill Carmichael and Deep River for your support and encouragement.

Finally, I would like to thank a man who has made an enormous impact on my life. He has done great things by living as an example to me and others—Steve Hampsch.

CONTENTS

CHAPTER 1

Great Things

"One of the main weaknesses of mankind is the average man's familiarity with the word 'impossible.' He knows all the rules which will not work. He knows all the things which cannot be done."

NAPOLEON HILL

I've always wondered what it would be like to do great things. I've watched countless History Channel specials and biography broadcasts about famous people in history who have done what the world generally considers to be great things. I've always admired the founding fathers of the United States, like George Washington, Benjamin Franklin, Thomas Jefferson, Alexander Hamilton, James Madison, and John Adams. I'm amazed at the incredible accomplishments of these leaders, in addition to the countless others who fought for and established the great nation of the United States.

I'm also amazed at the presidents over the years who successfully led our country through good times and bad. Presidents like Washington, Jefferson, Lincoln, Roosevelt, Eisenhower, Kennedy, and Reagan have intrigued me. Our nation continues to honor and revere these great leaders from our past, and rightfully so.

Likewise, I am inspired by the great accomplishments of people who have changed our world with their intelligence, talent, bravery, leadership, sacrifice, hard work, wisdom, and resolve. I think of Mother Teresa, Thomas Edison, Albert Einstein, Harriet Tubman, Neil Armstrong, Elvis Presley, Warren Buffett, Billy Graham, Babe Ruth, Sir Isaac Newton, Winston Churchill, Charles Lindbergh, Helen Keller, Martin Luther, Martin Luther King, Jr., Henry Ford. How's that for a list of amazing people?

I have played guitar for years, and I've always been fascinated by Eric Clapton. I am absolutely blown away when I see Clapton in concert. I am amazed at his outstanding talent for songwriting and singing, and by his incredible guitar-playing abilities. I have personally witnessed Eric Clapton doing great things as it relates to music and artistic expression.

I'm not alone in my fascination with people like these. But why are we so intrigued and obsessed with those who have done great things? What is it about their amazing accomplishments that we find so compelling? Perhaps there is a desire in each one of us that longs for greatness, something deep within our souls.

Have you ever considered your own capacity for great things? Do you believe you have the potential, ability, and will to capitalize on life's opportunities in order to fulfill your purpose?

Let me ask you another question: if you knew you could do whatever your heart was designed to do with complete fulfillment, excitement, passion, and adventure, without the possibility of failing, would you do it? I'm referring to the idea of living out of your true purpose, drinking from the well of real life. Keep in mind that I'm not asking you what others think you ought to be doing. No, I'm asking you to really ponder the idea of living life as you were designed to live it. I'm not suggesting a life with no difficulties or trials, and I'm not implying that it's possible to live in perfection. I'm describing a life grounded in authentic fulfillment.

If your answer is yes, then let's explore this idea further.

In the movie *Forrest Gump,* many lives were transformed because of the impact Forrest had on them, especially Jenny and Captain Dan. I think what I love most about the movie is that Forrest is an unlikely hero. Here's a man who has grown up with the odds stacked against him. He's not intelligent, and he has no father figure in his life. He didn't grow up in a wealthy home, and he struggles with several disabilities. Yet, despite all the setbacks, Forrest Gump lives an extraordinary life. He does great things, and he makes an enormous impact on the lives of those around him. Forrest finds himself in some devastating situations that include war, disaster, riots, personal disabilities, and a hurricane, and yet he emerges with incredible success while those around him can only see the negative circumstances. What a phenomenal story!

When we consider our heroes and amazing people, we don't typically think of people with the profile of Forrest Gump. No, our heroes and doers of great things should be attractive, intelligent, well educated, exciting, wealthy, privileged, and famous. John F. Kennedy, Jr. was the epitome of this description. Throughout his childhood and into adulthood, the press followed him, and many speculated that he would be a great leader, possibly even president of the United States. There are many who to this day question what amazing things JFK would have accomplished had his life not been cut short.

Why were such incredible expectations placed on this man? I believe it had more to do with his last name, wealth, background, and looks than it did with anything deeper.

How could such expectations be placed on anyone for such superficial reasons as those?

When I was growing up, there was no speculation from the media regarding my future. Reporters did not follow me to school and discuss what great things I might do in the future, and I would venture to say that they did not do so with you. In fact, at the time of writing this book, I am virtually unknown by any aside from my family and friends and acquaintances in the community where I live.

I grew up in an average, middle-class, blue-collar working family. I am a man of average intelligence and average looks. My grade-point average in grade school, high school, and college is not worth mentioning. I played soccer, but my athletic ability was average at best. My parents never attended college and were very young when they had me, so I did not have a wealth of resources at my disposal. Yet, having stated all those facts, I consider myself every bit as qualified for success as JFK was.

There are many in far worse situations than mine, with virtually no hope for a future, and there are millions in between with varied backgrounds, abilities, and potential. And then there are those with everything in the world at their disposal, including resources, talent, intelligence, and connections. This is the category we tend to expect the most from. The JFKs of the world. But the truth is your potential for success has very little to do with your background and abilities. In fact, your potential for success is determined by what you will do in the future as opposed to where you came from in the past.

In the following paragraphs, I'm going to outline a few scenarios, with real-life examples, of success or failure as they relate to roots and background. There is a great lesson to be learned in carefully examining background and its potential determination of a person's future.

Scenario 1:   A person is born into a virtually hopeless situation and yet emerges in success.

Isn't it fascinating when those with humble beginnings and virtually no hope for a future go on to do amazing things? It seems like a miracle when someone comes from such devastating circumstances and makes meaning out of his life. while those who have everything at their fingertips amount to very little in terms of contribution or personal fulfillment.

Abraham Lincoln is an excellent example of a man who lived an extraordinary life despite the fact that he was born into a very poor family. Lincoln was born in a one-room cabin in rural Kentucky in 1809, and he had a hard life growing up. He lost his mother at the age of nine, and he was not very close to his father. He was a self-educated man, and it goes without saying that Lincoln is considered to be one of the great US presidents. He was an inspiring leader who achieved great things despite many hardships and difficulties.[1]

Oprah Winfrey is another example of a person overcoming great obstacles. Oprah was born into poverty, and she was passed from family member to family member throughout her childhood. She was sexually abused multiple times by family members. At age fourteen, Oprah became pregnant, and she delivered a son who only lived for two weeks. Despite the terrible circumstances of her childhood, she went on to become one of the most popular and successful media stars in history.[2] Other examples abound. Richard Branson, a multibillion-dollar entrepreneur with over three hundred fifty companies under his control, was a high-school dropout, and he has dyslexia.[3] Michael Jordan, who many call one of the greatest basketball players to ever live, was cut from the high-school basketball team his sophomore year. Despite that setback, Jordan went on to win six NBA titles, one NCAA title, and two gold medals.[4]

Scenario 2:   A person is born into a virtually hopeless situation and never really emerges from the difficult environment.

Some people live out a self-fulfilling prophecy of failure and defeat. They never pull out of the environments they start from. They believe that there is no hope for them to go beyond where they are today, and they choose a life of fear, defeat, and emptiness.

We are typically not surprised at this situation—certainly not as surprised as we are when someone from such a background succeeds—because it seems more feasible that a person living in a negative environment will not have the means to rise above it. Some believe that the power of a person's environment is so overwhelming that it is nearly impossible to escape it.

During my childhood, I knew a boy from grade school who lived in a very troubling environment. He didn't know his father, and his mother didn't seem to care very much about him. He would wear the same clothes for months, and he did not bathe for days. He never did his homework, and he was always in trouble. He really didn't have anyone in his life who was providing him with any direction or hope for the future.

I got to know him a bit in seventh grade. He was a good kid despite his terrible circumstances, but unfortunately, he could no longer cope with his life, and he ended it with a gun one evening in the summer before our eighth-grade year.

This example is one of millions that exist in the world. I'm sure you can think of someone who has lived and possibly died in a similar fashion.

Scenario 3:   A person is born into (or eventually enters) an amazing environment, and yet chooses to squander it away.

Perhaps such people were born into a loving, caring family, or into a successful family by the world's standards. Despite having every opportunity and resource at their disposal, they waste their potential by living lives of "ignoble ease," as Theodore Roosevelt put it. In fact, President Roosevelt once said, "I wish to preach, not the doctrine of ignoble ease, but the doctrine of the strenuous life."[5]

I'm sure you've seen examples of children born into famous and wealthy families who end up addicted to drugs or who find themselves in and out of jail. Unfortunately, too many examples of this situation are playing out around us every day, and it seems to be growing more common.

There are also those who attain initial success or notoriety and go on to dismantle it later.

Whitney Houston is an example of someone who achieved a great deal early in her life. She is the only artist to chart seven consecutive number-one Billboard Hot 100 hits and seven consecutive multiplatinum albums. Whitney's combined albums, singles, and videos sold during her career with Arista Records totals 170 million. Her *Bodyguard* soundtrack is one of the top ten biggest-selling albums of all time at 17X platinum in just the United States alone, and her version of Dolly Parton's song "I Will Always Love You" is the biggest-selling United States single of all time. Whitney was born into an amazing musical family. Her mother was the well-known singer Cissy Houston, and her cousins Dee Dee Warwick and Dionne Warwick were both successful artists. All had an influential impact on Whitney. Whitney found success as a singer in her teenage years with performances in the 1970s and early 1980s with stars such as Chaka Khan, the Neville Brothers, and others. When she was twenty-one, Whitney's first album debuted with over twelve million copies sold in the United States, and it set the record as the biggest-selling debut album by a solo artist. Music historians say Whitney may have had the greatest voice of our time.[6]

Whitney Houston was fortunate to be born into such an amazing musical family. She was also born with an unbelievable voice, and she had the advantage of musical connections and influences. She experienced amazing success early in her career because she took action and capitalized on her potential. She worked extremely hard, and she did not waste any opportunity. However, she came to a point in her life when things began to change. Allegations of drug use and unpredictable behavior became the headlines in the news in place of the accolades and stunning reviews. In an unfortunate series of events, Whitney's career and life came to a premature end. I wonder what Whitney could have continued to do had she not wasted such amazing potential.[7]

In addition, it seems like you can't turn on the news without hearing about a child of a celebrity going terribly wrong. Celebrity children seem to struggle more than the rest of us with drugs, alcohol, arrest, and suicide. Marie Osmond, Paul Newman, Art Linkletter, and many other celebrities have lost children to drug overdoses or suicide. True, whether it's really a benefit to be the child of someone famous can be argued, but it's certainly difficult to make a negative case against a backdrop of children who are born with no family or into extreme poverty.

Scenario 4:   A person is born into a great environment with outstanding opportunities and resources at his fingertips, and he chooses to do great things. He decides to commit to things greater than himself.

Steve Forbes is an example of a man born into great promise and potential who capitalized on that potential. His grandfather founded Forbes, Inc., in 1917. Forbes was well educated and took over a flourishing business that had been established for some time. There are many who wish for an opportunity like he had. Others do share his advantages, yet, perhaps due to the intimidation of high expectations, they never step to the plate and really make the attempt. Steve Forbes, on the other hand, has done great things. Forbes's career and accomplishments speak volumes. Under Forbes's leadership, his company has launched countless publications and businesses across the world. *Forbes* magazine has become the nation's leading business magazine with an international audience in excess of six million readers. In addition, Forbes served in the Reagan and George W. Bush administrations as chairman of the board for international broadcasting, he has authored several books, and serves on several prominent boards. I recently attended a luncheon at which Steve Forbes was the guest speaker, and I was impressed with his knowledge and perspective on capitalism, politics, and the world in general. He has certainly done great things.[8]

Other examples of people born into amazing environments who go on to accomplish great things include Peyton and Eli Manning, sons of the great football player Archie Manning, who have become pro players as well. Michael Douglas, son of the famous actor Kirk Douglas, went on to become a star in his own right. Actress Kate Hudson, the daughter of Goldie Hawn and Keifer Sutherland (himself the son of Donald Sutherland) is another example.

The point I am making in these scenarios must be understood as a foundation for your life. It is a concept and worldview that can transform your very life and the way you live it. Simply put, your circumstances, your background, your experience, your intelligence, your family history, your mistakes, your accomplishments, your education, your lack of education and so on *do not and cannot dictate what you choose to do with your future.*

I don't care if you were born into excellent circumstances or extreme poverty or abuse, you have the potential and possibility to do great things. You have the power to shape your future.

Many people have already made life decisions about themselves based on bad data. They have already decided who they are and what they are capable of. There are many who have made these decisions quite early in the lives, as if their lives are predetermined in some way. The amazing thing about this mindset is that most people are unaware of the fact that they have it!

Scenario 5:   This is your scenario. You were born into a unique situation and environment that is not exactly the same as anyone else's who has ever lived. It might be similar, but it is not exactly the same. But even more than that, you have the potential to do great things. Your potential for greatness has very little to do with your background or where you came from.

My junior year in college, I had the opportunity to apply for an internship with a large, successful, and well-respected company that was headquartered near my school. There were two positions available, and these two positions were the highest paying, most prestigious of all the internships available in my field. Several of my classmates were applying, and there was a lot of discussion about who would be chosen for these two positions. I found out that there were several hundred applicants, and they would have the opportunity to interview over the course of several days.

On the second-to-last day of interviewing, one of my professors approached me on campus and asked if I would be interviewing for the internship. I was surprised—shocked, in fact—by her question. I had no intention of subjecting myself to the interview. I was a C student with no credentials or promise of attaining such a position. Considering I had attended several of her classes, she should have known that I wasn't qualified! I had barely passed her classes in the past, and I wasn't doing so well in the class she was teaching at the time.

Do you see how I had already made decisions about who I was and what I was capable of? I was only twenty years old, and I already had strong limiting beliefs about who I was and what I could and could not do. If you'd asked me outright about those beliefs, I would never have admitted them. I really wasn't fully aware I believed them, yet I was making decisions based on them.

My professor encouraged me to interview on the last day. She even wrote a recommendation—I needed it because my grade-point average did not meet the required standard to be accepted for the interview. I reluctantly agreed to take it. I was reluctant because I didn't want to put myself in an embarrassing situation. I didn't want to be let down. Maybe there was part of me that did not want confirmation of what I already believed to be true.

How about you? Are you taking yourself out of the game? Are you thinking to yourself, "You can't lose if you don't play"? As I look back on it now, I know that's what I was doing: I was taking myself out of the game as it related to my performance academically. It was much easier to take a C grade knowing that I hadn't really tried that hard. You too may be taking yourself out of the game, and you may not even realize what you are doing or why.

When you put yourself on the line and give it everything you have, then you truly know if you have what it takes or not. I was afraid to know that answer.

On the last day of interviewing, I showed up and did the interview. I was shocked when I was called back for a second and then a third. A week later, I received a phone call: they had selected me to make my choice of the two positions. I couldn't believe it. My professor and several employees of the hiring company believed in me more than I believed in myself. I had the internship!

My professor later shared with me that she knew I had potential, but I needed to start trying or else that potential would be wasted. She asked me if my grade-point average truly reflected my abilities and potential. They did not. But my future was not to be dictated by my past. I had established a new belief about myself, and that is where real change and accomplishment begin.

To accomplish great things in your life, I'm not asking you to be become someone different. Make no mistake about it. I am not encouraging you to become someone else. How many times have you looked at someone else and thought to yourself, "I wish I could be more like that person"? Have you ever dreamed of changing your personality and morphing into a completely different person? How many times have you quietly said to yourself,

- If only I were smarter
- If only I were funny
- If only I had different parents, or a different spouse, or a different job
- If only the economy were better
- If only I had more money

To do great things, you do not need to become someone you are not. Rather, you are about to embark on an amazing journey and incredible adventure, starting with a foundation of self-discovery that will lead to accomplishing great things. That foundation is based on principles and truth, and while we will explore techniques and exercises aimed at shaping your potential, our foundation will be on truth and God's principles. Techniques have value when they are practiced on a solid foundation of truth; however, when used outside God's will, they are simply gimmicks and tricks that will ultimately fall short.

I recently purchased a 1960 Corvette. It has been my dream car since I was a small child. I've spent years looking for the right combination, and during that time, I've looked at a lot of 1960 Corvettes. One day I thought I had found the perfect car. On the outside, the car was in fantastic condition. The paint was incredible; the interior was perfect. It was a real "head turner."

Before I would purchase the car, I had an inspection to ensure it was in good working condition. After a thorough examination of the car, it was determined that the frame was not solid. This car was rusting away from the inside. Even though the exterior was flawless, the car could be dangerous on the road because the integrity of the frame was in question.

Many in the world today are living just like that Corvette. They are great at looking good on the outside. As far as appearances go, they've got everyone thinking they've got it together. But while they're occupied with appearance, status, and what other people think, they struggle to find real meaning and purpose in their lives. They're living in fear of others finding out who they really are. They're doing just enough to get by, and they're afraid to ever really take a chance on anything—especially on themselves.

I could have purchased that Corvette with the rusty frame, and I might even have made some modifications, like a new stereo system or custom interior or different wheels, but those improvements would have been a complete waste without a solid foundation. What difference does it make if you have an awesome stereo system in a car that has broken in half?

So the question becomes, what is a solid foundation? (And I'm not talking about a Corvette.) What does that even mean? Is it self-confidence? Is it a lack of fear? Is it peace? Is it real understanding of myself? Does it mean that I'm willing to take chances? Is it a belief in myself?

We'll explore this question in more detail as we go, but in a nutshell, the solid foundation for your life is a belief system based on truth and the discovery of who you were designed to be so that you can realize your purpose, potential, and abilities as designed by God.

I have found that the things which I learn on my own, those things which I internalize and truly understand, revolutionize my life in a dramatic way. Why? Because I am the one who made the discovery. Dr. Howard Hendricks, a great professor of theology, says, "Knowledge that is self-discovered is stored in the deepest part of the mind and remains the longest in memory. There is no jewel more precious than that which you have mined yourself."

I promise that if you are willing to open your mind and seek the real truth of who you are, you will make a discovery that will dramatically change your life. You will understand the foundation upon which an amazing life can be built. You will go on to do great things. These things will be the fruit of that foundation, and they will impact you and everyone around you in a dynamic way. This will be an epiphany of enormous proportions.

Once you have the foundation, great things will flow naturally from your life.

You will not miss it if you desire to know it, though your definition of "great things" might change as you continue to read. Let's take a moment and define what great things are. I'll start first by defining what they are not. Great things are not:

- Fame
- Fortune
- Self-gratification
- Accumulation of things
- Power
- Popularity

Our culture today has confused and twisted things around. Although fame and fortune and power are not inherently bad, they are completely irrelevant to authentic great things. Many in history have obtained fame and fortune and power and popularity, but they did not do great things. Adolf Hitler is one example of this truth. I think most would agree that these things are not the ingredients to greatness, although they are confused for greatness every day.

You currently have the potential to do amazing things in the situation where you reside. I am talking about things of real value and meaning. I'm talking about things that get you excited, those of great adventure, risk, and danger. I'm talking about things that scare you to death and thrill you all at the same time.

As I already shared, I am the quintessential average person. However, I am living an extraordinary life. I'm not doing so because I'm somehow more special than others. I'm not a great or amazing person, but I am doing great and amazing things. I'm fulfilled, I'm happy, and I live an adventure every day. Oh, I have my moments and struggles like everyone else. Things do not come easily to me. I have to work extremely hard. I'm an imperfect person with many flaws, but I am doing great things.

I gave my life to Jesus Christ at a very young age, and I grew up going through times of obedience and times of rebellion. I married my high-school sweetheart, Angie, and I am more in love with her today than I ever was when we first married. I can't wait to get home and see her at the end of the day. I love sharing my deepest thoughts with her, and I love hearing what she thinks.

We have four children, and I have the opportunity to be their daddy every single day. I make a lot of mistakes, but they always forgive me. I love my family, and I just love spending time with them. Each of my children absolutely amazes me. They are all different in their own way.

I am blessed with many great friends. My friends stand by me even when I mess up, and they are the first ones to point me back in the right direction.

I have the opportunity to serve in many ways at the church I belong to. Despite my shortcomings, I am involved in people's lives, and I love it. I have the opportunity to teach an adult Sunday school class. I serve in various capacities within the church where my strengths and abilities are the strongest. I thoroughly enjoy serving even though I'm not a natural "giver."

I also serve in my community in civic service, and I'm able to contribute back to the wonderful city that we call home.

I'm an entrepreneur. I love to take chances. I've started several businesses from scratch and built them up, and I've had the opportunity to sell them. There are many people out there who are much better at business than me, but I've had good success despite that fact. Although I've been fortunate in my business dealings, I understand that I can fail at any time. Failure doesn't paralyze me any-more. My self-worth has nothing do with my successes or failures.

I'm the average Joe who's living a life of great things. I'm blessed beyond measure, and I wake up every day thanking God for everything he has done for me. I'm genuinely happy, although I have my share of bad days. My circum-stances have little to do with my joy. I'm confident in myself, but that confidence does not rest on my abilities, strength, achievements, or anything that I do. It's tethered to something far greater.

That something is the real foundation of success, the real foundation of a life worth living. Take a moment and consider that God does exist. If God does exist and he created the entire universe, including you, then he knows exactly how you are wired. He has knowledge regarding what can truly fulfill you. He knows bet-ter than anyone in the world, including yourself, what makes you happy and what makes you tick. In fact, not only does he know what makes you tick, but he's the reason you are wired the way you are. It was his design from the very beginning.

Think about it. Aren't there things that you thoroughly enjoy doing today that you never could have imagined enjoying years ago? I started playing guitar my freshman year in college. Through the years I've played in a few bands, and I have loved every minute of it. If you asked me in high school if I would enjoy playing guitar in a band, I wouldn't have even considered it. I had no idea at that time in my life that I would enjoy making music or playing a musical instrument. In fact, several years ago I really immersed myself into blues music, and I even played in an exclusive blues band for a couple of years. I didn't even know what blues music was in high school, and I would never have guessed I'd be that pas-sionate about it. On the other hand, God knows exactly what you will love doing in the future. He knows the very things that can fulfill you completely, even though you are completely oblivious to those things now.

Now imagine for a moment that you could access that information. Your self-discovery would be off the charts. I'm not saying that things would be easy or per-fect, but most great things aren't easy. I'd also like to point out that God is more interested in your character development and who you are than he is in your level of comfort. I can truly identify with this concept after becoming a father. I enjoy watching my kids have a great time, but I also know that it is important that they learn and grow and acquire the necessary skills for success. It is essential for their future.

A few years ago, two of my sons were fighting with each other, and I stepped in to break it up. The younger brother was doing everything he could to annoy his older brother, and I must say he was very successful in this endeavor. I pulled my older son to the side and gave him some advice on how to deal with it. I had a younger brother growing up, so I had some experience in this area.

A few hour hours later another dispute broke out, and I could see the younger brother was back in full stride. I could have stepped in immediately and broken it up, but I waited. I wanted to see how my older son would handle the situation now that he was armed with my advice.

God does the same sometimes. He allows us to go through a trial or difficult situation, because he cares more about our character than our comfort.

So if God knows exactly what makes us tick, and he loves us, doesn't it make sense to align with his plan for our lives instead of stumbling around on our own like a blind squirrel in search of a nut?

Stephen Covey writes, "Begin with the End in Mind means to begin each day, task, or project with a clear vision of your desired direction and destination."[9] God will not always reveal his entire plan for us upfront, so it will not always be possible to have clear understanding of your destination, but I guarantee you that his plan is the only way to be fulfilled. His plan is the only one that will lead any-where meaningful. Significance outside of God's plan is a myth, and you will never know God's plan without a relationship with God.

With that relationship as your foundation, you can use the principles of God's Word to live an extraordinary life—a life that only *you* are designed to live.

Over the last decade, I've spent considerable time researching the great entre-preneurs of America. I have been fascinated by the idea that each entrepreneur is unique and creative in his or her own specific way. Every great entrepreneur has a unique style, background, ability, and approach. I was amazed to discover the varied personalities, experience, and education in their stories.

As I started to look deeper, I began to discover common threads of behavior present in the great entrepreneurs. I realized that there were certain principles or methods that these great entrepreneurs were employing in their ventures that were instrumental to their success, regardless of their background, experience, education, or personality type.

I also discovered that these entrepreneurial methods could be applied and used in one's personal life with remarkable results. For example, the great entre-preneurs are able to see opportunity that others don't typically see, and they have an ability to capitalize on those opportunities in creative and trailblazing ways. The great entrepreneurs are excellent at creating vision and inspiring others to that particular vision. They are driven, efficient, and passionate about what they do. They are able to overcome their fears and actually use fear to their advantage. They have a sense for what's really important, and they tend to focus on the right things. The great entrepreneurs are good at evaluating options while minimizing risk and maximizing opportunity, and they have a sixth sense for anticipating trends. They have resolve and persistence, and they are great at turning defeat into opportunity.

Throughout this book, you will learn the process of applying these entrepreneurial methods in your own personal life. You will be amazed at the potential that you already possess when you start to apply these amazing methods.

While these entrepreneurial methods have incredible value, they are simply a collection of contrived techniques without the foundation of Christian principles. I can provide countless examples of great entrepreneurs who have amassed outrageous fortunes only to find that they are not fulfilled and are living a meaningless existence without an authentic foundation.

If you build your life on techniques and manipulation in a self-serving approach to get as much as you can, I can assure you that a great awakening will occur in your life at some point. Unfortunately, this happens for many people near the end of their lives when it's too late. The Bible says, "What good is it for a man to gain the whole world, yet forfeit his soul?"[10] John D. Rockefeller, perhaps one of the wealthiest men in history, was once asked, "How much money is enough money?" Rockefeller replied, "Just a little bit more."[11]

If you have no interest in God and spiritual things, I would like to make a deal with you as you continue reading this book. I encourage you to complete the book on the basis of learning and applying the powerful entrepreneurial methods that are presented. The value of these methods will pay significant dividends in your personal life. As you encounter the references to God, consider the possibility that these references represent an area you should perhaps reconsider. Keep an open mind and really think through these areas of your life. You may be surprised, and you might possibly make a discovery that could transform your entire life. Think about it for a moment: if what you are believing or not believing right now is not true, do you want to know the truth? If your answer really is yes, you owe it to yourself to keep an open mind.

What you are about to read will light a fire for change in your life, because you are about to embark on a journey. Maybe you find yourself escaping to a world that does not resemble reality. Many people escape in their own minds where they live out their fantasies and dreams, never knowing or realizing those thoughts as reality. Perhaps you spend more time daydreaming about who you want to be than really living.

Incredible opportunity exists for you as you read further, and I am excited for what you will discover. My mission in writing this book is this: I seek to inspire, motivate and equip you to find authentic fulfillment, passion, and meaning by truly discovering the exact person God made you to be while applying amazing entrepreneurial methods in your life.

I believe every person on earth has incredible value and potential, and when a person understands his or her purpose, potential, and abilities as designed by God, that person will accomplish and experience great things.

The amazing thing about this journey of great things is that you are the only person in the world right now who can accomplish your purpose. There is no one else who can step into your shoes and be you better than you can be you. At this very moment of your life, you must decide. Who are you? What is your purpose? What are the great things that you've been called to? I'm so excited about the adventure before you.

CHAPTER 2

Creating a Climate for Change

"When we are no longer able to change a situation—we are challenged to change ourselves."

VIKTOR FRANKL

When I was eight or nine years old, my family vacationed throughout the summer months at a state park campground in Piedmont, Missouri, called Clear Water Lake. I learned to water ski at a young age, and I spent every possible moment behind the boat on a pair of skis. I can still vividly recall those moments on the water with my family. It was a dramatic sight to look out at the deep blue lake turning to brilliant white as the sun hit it just right and the breathtaking rock bluffs surrounding the lake in beautiful Ozark country.

I always loved the feeling of climbing into the boat after hours in the water to feel the heat of the sun warming my body and the wind in my hair as our boat carried us back to the campground.

I also loved the idea of being with my family. My grandfather, Hadley, started waterskiing around the same time I learned, and we both progressed a little each summer. We each learned to do new things on skis, and we became very competitive. It became a fun contest to see who could master new moves on our water skis first.

During this particular summer, I recall one maneuver that neither of us could quite pull off. We were both in a heated competition to be the first to cross the boat wake. This move consisted of leaning out and pushing off in order to guide our skis over the wake of the boat.

My grandfather and I tried all summer long to be the first to do it. My dad demonstrated how to do it over and over again. My entire family was giving me all kinds of advice, and then there was my grandfather. I couldn't let him cross that wake before I did! I remember making attempt after attempt until my legs couldn't hold up any longer.

As the summer neared its end in late August, I started to think I would never cross the wake. My grandfather had yet to accomplish it either, and I really doubted if we would ever do it.

On our last trip of the summer, I recall giving it one last try. I quickly got up on my skis, and I immediately pushed off to cross the wake in hopes of making it while my legs were still fresh. As I was struggling and straining, I closed my eyes and silently insisted that I *would* cross the wake. I would give it everything I had inside me. In the chaos and spray of the water from the boat, I thought for a moment that I had crossed. I remember opening my eyes in great anticipation only to find I was still behind the boat, having not crossed at all. I let go of the rope and slowly sank into the cool blue water. That was it. I finally concluded that I could not do it. I would try no longer.

The next day we were back in the boat, and my grandfather was skiing. He was still in the hunt for success, despite my concession. My grandfather was not someone who gave up easily. He had served in the US Army Air Corps at the end of World War II in Japan, and as a crop duster pilot, he survived a death-defying crash in 1959. He broke every bone in his body and was laid up in a hospital for fourteen months. Despite this life-changing setback, here he was on water skis twenty years later.

He continued to make several attempts, and then something amazing happened. Out of nowhere, he crossed the wake. I remember seeing a look of disbelief on his face as his skis rode up and over the other side. We were all yelling and screaming from the boat, and he was elated.

As soon as my grandfather finished his run, I immediately hit the water again. This time something was different. I realized that it was possible, and I had to give it one last shot. I remember my grandfather yelling from the boat as they circled around me to get into position, "Aaron, you can do it. If I can do it, you can do it."

Within moments, the boat started accelerating and I was up. I starting cutting as the boat struggled to plane out. I began to feel the push of the wake almost taunting me. I started to cut harder, and in an instant my skis burst right through the wake and I found myself on the other side. I can't even begin to explain the incredible feeling of elation that came over me! After months of trying and failing and trying and failing, I had crossed the wake.

As soon as I'd done it, I crossed back to the middle and began crossing back and forth with ease. How in the world was it possible that I had crossed just moments after my grandfather, considering we were making attempts all summer long? Was it just coincidence that we both happened to cross at virtually the same time?

This phenomenon is not unique to that particular situation. It has to do with a change in mindset, or what is called a *paradigm shift*.

My grandfather and I crossed the exact same wake within minutes of each other behind the same boat in the same lake, but we crossed for different reasons. My grandfather crossed because he did not give up, and his sheer determination and resolve motivated him to keep trying until the goal was achieved. He always believed that he would make it if he just kept trying.

I, on the other hand, crossed the wake because my belief about whether I could cross had changed dramatically based on my grandfather's experience. My entire mindset changed in an instant as I watched my grandfather cross. I experienced a paradigm shift. Once my paradigm shifted, I crossed the wake with ease, exerting less effort than in my previous attempts.

In a much more publicized event in 1954, a similar thing happened when a man named Roger Bannister accomplished something thought to be impossible. Prior to this event, the entire world considered it impossible for a human being to run a mile in under four minutes. The world record at that time was 4:01.3, and that record stood for nine years. Medical doctors stated that it was not possible for a human body to break the four-minute barrier. Countless athletes tried their best to prove them wrong, but to no avail.

Roger Bannister, a young medical student and amateur runner, announced to the world in the early 1950s that he would break the four-minute barrier. Many scoffed at his ambitious announcement and considered it impossible. The world's greatest runners had been attempting this feat for centuries with incredible effort, but with no success.

On May 6, 1954, Roger Bannister shocked the world when he ran a mile in the record breaking time of 3:59.4 in Oxford, England. Bannister actually accomplished the run with a fifteen-mile-per-hour crosswind. His incredible accomplishment demonstrated the power of determination and resolve in addition to hard work and discipline.[1] But something amazing happened after Bannister shattered the supposed insurmountable record. Seven weeks later, John Landy, an Australian, broke Bannister's record by also running a mile in under four minutes.

It is reported that sixteen people ran a mile in under four minutes within just three years of Bannister's doing it for the first time. How is it possible that a barrier that was so impossible to cross was crushed by over a dozen different people in just a few years? Is it a coincidence that Roger Bannister and John Landy would achieve such an amazing accomplishment just weeks apart? How can we explain that another sixteen people accomplished this same amazing run within just three years of Bannister's first record run?[2]

Maybe a new running shoe came to market in 1954 that made it possible? Perhaps a new energy drink was created that gave the runners the extra boost they needed to break the four-minute mile? The answer is no. Something else happened that created the phenomenon. *Roger Bannister proved to the world that it was possible to run a mile in under four minutes, and then paradigms were shifted.* John Landy's belief system was altered. People no longer believed it was impossible, and they started to think and act differently.

Creating a Paradigm Shift

Stephen Covey wrote about the phenomenon of a *paradigm shift* in his ground-breaking book, *The 7 Habits of Highly Effective People.* Covey dramatically increased the worldwide awareness of the term *paradigm,* which he defines this way: "In the more general sense, it's the way we 'see' the world—not in terms of our visual sense of sight, but in terms of perceiving, understanding, interpreting."[3]

In short, a paradigm is your own set of beliefs about something. In the broader sense, it's how you believe the world works. A paradigm is your own mental picture of how you believe things are.

Paradigms are not always aligned with reality, and in many cases, they have no basis in reality whatsoever. Yet, a person's paradigm influences behavior and thought.

For example, when I was sixteen years old, I believed I was indestructible, as many sixteen-year-old boys do. This paradigm was mostly rooted in my subconscious mind. I didn't go around telling people I was indestructible, but my actions clearly communicated my paradigm. I drove my cars extremely fast. I used to "hood surf" with friends on the weekends. Hood surfing was an activity that included sitting on the hood of a car, with your back to the windshield, while holding on for your life. I had friends who drove me up to speeds of sixty miles per hour with me sitting on the hood of their car.

Today, you couldn't pay me a million dollars to hood surf on anyone's car. Why? My paradigm has shifted. As I've gotten older, I've learned that life is fragile and accidents happen every day. As my paradigm has shifted, my behaviors and thoughts have also shifted to reflect my new beliefs. Our paradigms change as we get older and we learn through experience—yet we continue to hold many paradigms despite their destructive natures.

Rather than fact, our paradigms are often based on perception. We tend to base our conclusions in life on our own thoughts and reasoning. The results are not always positive. The Bible says, "There is a way that appears to be right, but in the end it leads to death."[4]

You may believe in something with every fiber of your being, but that does not make it true. Several thousand years ago, most people in the world believed the world to be flat. If polls were taken in that day and age, the results would be overwhelming for the belief that the world was flat. Yet the popularity of that belief and the conviction of those supporting that belief did not make the paradigm true.

We later discovered the world to be round. Once that paradigm changed, behavior also changed. For centuries, most ships sailed close to land's edge for fear that they would fall off the end of the earth. New discoveries, continents, and beliefs about the universe came to light after the world's paradigm shifted.

What paradigms do you currently have that are limiting your potential in some way? It's an interesting question. Many paradigms that we hold to are part of our subconscious minds, and we are not even aware of their power and influence.

You may believe that you are not loved. You might feel that you really don't have any abilities or talents. Maybe you question your purpose in life, and you really don't know who you are. Consider the impact of these paradigms. If you have paradigms that do not correspond to reality, then you are probably taking action that runs contrary to what's really best for you.

Henry Ford once said, "If you think you can do a thing or think you can't do a thing, you're right." Our paradigms in many ways become self-fulfilling prophecy.

Stephen Covey uses an analogy of a map to describe accurate and inaccurate paradigms. He explains that a map is a model or guide to a particular territory:

Suppose you wanted to arrive at a specific location in central Chicago. A street map of the city would be a great help to you in reaching your destination. But suppose you were given the wrong map. Through a printing error, the map labeled, "Chicago" was actually a map of Detroit. Can you imagine the frustration, the ineffectiveness of trying to reach your destination? You might work on your *behavior*—you could try harder, be more diligent, double your speed. But your efforts would only succeed in getting you to the wrong place faster. You might work on your *attitude*—you could think more positively. You still wouldn't get to the right place.[5]

Consider for a moment that your current maps (or paradigms) about yourself are inaccurate. Is it possible that you are holding on to beliefs and ideas about yourself and the world around you that are simply not true? What kind of effect is that having on your life?

If you believe that you can never really be successful, how effective will you be in your career field or business? What if you have a paradigm that says you'll never really be loved unconditionally? What effect will that belief system have on your marriage, friendships, relationship to God? What if you believe that you can achieve a certain measure of success, but it is not possible to experience extraordinary success? What if your paradigm says you are not smart? How well will you do in school?

What if your beliefs about God or the existence of God are inaccurate? What if your understanding of real truth is not in line with real truth? How will that affect your life? What if your paradigm says that only bad things happen to you? What if you believe you are unlucky and things never go your way?

If your paradigm is inaccurate, you are set up for failure before you even begin. When I was trying to cross that wake on my water skis, I had a paradigm that said it wasn't possible. It didn't matter how hard I tried.

How can you explain sixteen people running a mile in under four minutes just a few years after Roger Bannister did it for the first time? I would bet those people had inaccurate paradigms that said it wasn't possible until Bannister obliterated their paradigms by crushing the four-minute barrier.

Your understanding and use of this incredible concept can have a dramatic influence in the direction and course of your life. A simple change in your paradigm about how you see yourself can literally change your entire life. It can have lasting impact, and it can alter your life and the lives around you.

The power of the mind is an amazing thing, and you are about to embark on a journey of monumental proportions. We are going to explore the incredible power of a paradigm alteration in the most important areas of your life. A paradigm shift has the potential to not only change your entire life, but to impact the lives of people around you and all over the world as well.

The world today consists of a lot of people who simply go through the motions of life. Most people simply react to the circumstances before them without any hope for something more. This usually occurs when people have unknowingly concluded that there is nothing more than what is visible before them.

Napoleon Hill stated, "Ninety-eight out of every hundred people working for wages today are in the positions they hold because they lacked the definiteness of decision to plan a definite position, and the knowledge of how to choose an employer."

I believe this truth applies to much more than just career choices. I went through an incredible paradigm shift in my own life as it related to my career. Several years ago, I was working in a job that I did not enjoy. I always dreamed of being a successful entrepreneur. I had a strong desire to start and own my own business, but I had several issues internally that I had to deal with. I had paradigms that were limiting me, and I wasn't even aware of their effect on my life. I agonized about the fact that I was still working for someone else despite my incredible passion to start a business. My internal map about what I was capable of did not align with what I dreamed of doing.

Then one day, I experienced a life-changing paradigm shift that altered everything about my own beliefs regarding my potential. (I write about this in more detail in the chapter on fear.) Within six months of my paradigm shifting, I started my first business, and I've never looked back.

Over the years, I have accomplished more than I ever imagined or thought possible. But hold on for just a moment. I don't want you to get the wrong idea about me. My success actually has nothing to do with me being an entrepreneur. It actually has more to do with me becoming who God designed me to be.

Once my paradigm shifted and my beliefs aligned with God's intentions for my life, everything changed. That's not surprising, since the Bible describes God this way: "Now to him who is able to do immeasurably more than all we ask or imagine, according to his power that is at work within us."[6]

Unfortunately we often judge success and failure based on outward appearances. The fact is that I could have experienced incredible failure in my business ventures, and my own value and worth to God would be exactly the same as they are today. It is possible that I may go completely broke in the future, but my value and worth to God will not change. In fact, future failures may be incredible learning opportunities for something even greater.

My paradigm about who I am and how God has made me changed dramatically when I realized that I could accomplish anything if I was at the center of God's will. It wasn't until I realized this truth that I started to enjoy the incredible pleasure of being at the center of God's will and living in complete fulfillment.

I also learned that my life is not one-dimensional. Today, I am a husband, a father, a son, a brother, a business owner and entrepreneur, a Sunday school teacher, a friend, and an author. Our paradigms must accurately reflect all the components of our lives in order for us to truly experience the incredible plans God has for us. I have a strong desire to be the best husband and father that I can possibly be. I would never want to short-circuit my role as a husband in order to accomplish success as an entrepreneur.

Unfortunately, many people today operate with a paradigm that says they must sacrifice everything in order to succeed in one area. When our paradigms align with God's plans, we become equipped for amazing experiences. The Bible says, "For I know the plans I have for you, declares the LORD, plans to prosper you and not to harm you, plans to give you hope and a future."[7] God has specific plans for you, and they are amazing plans for your future. You must divorce yourself of your own plans and adopt God's plans instead. They are far greater than anything you can possibly imagine. Any plans that you have made for yourself that God was not a party to are of the world and are inferior in every way to God's perfect plans for your life. If you really begin to believe that God's plans are better than yours, that paradigm shift alone will have a dramatic effect on your life.

God has made you for great adventure, but misaligned paradigms can box you in and keep you from being fulfilled. If you have a paradigm that says your worth is derived from what other people think of you, then your behavior and actions will be dictated by that mindset. You might spend all your energy and efforts in trying to look good and give an appearance of success in the absence of authentic fulfillment and meaning.

Our paradigms dictate what we do and how we live. If you have a paradigm that says the only way to have fun is with drugs and alcohol, then I have a good idea of what you are doing on the weekends.

If you have a paradigm that says the only way to the top is by stepping on other people to get there, then I would be willing to bet you will be stepping on other people.

If you have a paradigm that says God is out to get you and he only wants to make your life miserable, then you probably will not be seeking his guidance in your life.

If you have a paradigm that says there is no such thing as true friendship and everyone will eventually stab you in the back, then you probably will not have any close, meaningful friendships.

If you have a paradigm that says hard work is a waste of time and having fun is more important, then you are probably living in chaos.

ALIGNING YOUR PARADIGMS TO REALITY

The important thing to consider as you dissect your beliefs is to figure out what you are basing those beliefs on. What evidence are you using to come to a particular conclusion? Someone once shared with me that he believed in reincarnation. I told him that I respected his opinion, but I was curious what evidence he was basing that belief on. He couldn't give me any evidence. He just had a feeling that seemed right to him.

I urge you to start validating your beliefs with evidence and reason. If you are going to adopt a belief, and you will make life-altering decisions based on that belief, you'd better base that belief on more than a ten-second thought or feeling!

Chuck Colson wrote about a similar situation in his book *The Faith*. He was attending an exclusive dinner the night before a governor's prayer breakfast. He writes:

The gentleman seated next to me greeted me with a blunt warning that he was an atheist. I looked at him for a moment—graying temples, a wise expression, handsomely attired—the very image of a community leader. I told him I was glad to sit next to him because I've never really met an atheist.

As his eyebrows arched, I explained, "An atheist believes the existence of God can be disproved. So please, tell me how you've done that." He looked momentarily uncomfortable. "Well, perhaps I should say I'm an agnostic."

"When did you give up studying about God?" I asked.

Now his neck began to redden. He admitted he'd really never tried.

"But an agnostic is one who says he doesn't think God can be known, and you can only be an agnostic if you've tried to know Him and exhausted the search." I'm not sure even now what made me so bold, but I added, "So I would say that while you appear to be a very well-educated person, you've made an unsupportable statement."[8]

How many beliefs do you have right now that are unsupportable? It's a tough question, but I have to ask. The very idea of thinking through our belief systems can have a profound effect on our lives.

Colson actually received some feedback from his encounter a few weeks later:

Some weeks later I received a copy of the editorial page of the state's largest newspaper. It turned out my dinner companion was the publisher. His lead editorial was an explanation of how my visit had affected his view of life, how religion was indeed an important element of all our lives and something we needed to pursue. What struck the publisher was that his own point of view proved unsupportable.[9]

Isn't it amazing that this man was willing to reconsider his belief system, his paradigm about life and God? I admire such a move. It shows real character and humble openness to evaluate our beliefs and why we believe them. And it's imperative that we do. It's so important because those paradigms are influencing what we do every day.

A POWERFUL PARADIGM YIELDS AMAZING RESULTS

I've always been amazed at Joseph from the Bible. I believe his paradigm about who he was and how God was involved in his life were exactly aligned with reality. Joseph's great-grandfather was Abraham. Joseph was the eleventh son of Jacob, and he was the favorite of his father. When he was only a teenager, his older brothers sold him into slavery. In order to cover up their deeds, the brothers told their father that Joseph had been killed by a wild animal.

Joseph ended up in Egypt working under Potiphar, one of Pharaoh's officials. During this time, the Bible says, "The Lord was with Joseph so that he prospered, and he lived in the house of his Egyptian master. When his master saw that the Lord was with him and that the Lord gave him success in everything he did… Potiphar put him in charge of his household, and he entrusted to his care everything he owned."[10]

Joseph prospered, found success, and did great things despite his situation. Think about this for moment. Why did Joseph prosper? Answer: The Lord was with Joseph. Why was the Lord with Joseph? Joseph's paradigm was aligned with God's plan for his life. He allowed God to be in control instead of the other way around.

After a while, Potiphar's wife began making advances toward Joseph. She really put the pressure on, but Joseph refused to sleep with her. After several attempts, she falsely accused Joseph of making advances toward her, and Joseph was thrown into prison. Now let me ask another question. Couldn't God have intervened and not allowed this to happen? Sure, but God is more concerned with our character than our comfort.

Once Joseph ended up in prison, you would think he'd had enough. He had been obedient and never turned from God, but things were not going his way. He could have made a million excuses for cursing God, but he did not. The Bible says, "But while Joseph was there in prison, the Lord was with him; He showed him kindness and granted him favor in the eyes of the prison warden."[11]

In fact, the warden put Joseph in charge of the entire prison. It is clear that Joseph could do great things. Those great things were based on a foundation, a belief system that was unwavering. After several years, Joseph found himself directly under Pharaoh.

At the age of thirty, Joseph was placed over the entire land of Egypt. He was a man of action. He knew who he was and whom he depended on. Can't you just sense his confidence as you hear his story? I'm talking about a confidence in God, not a confidence in his own abilities.

During Joseph's command of Egypt, he created and oversaw a plan that saved millions of lives from a seven-year famine, including his own family. His own brothers came face-to-face with him years after selling him into slavery, and they acknowledged that he was responsible for saving them.

Think about the paradigms that Joseph had. His circumstances did not control his actions, and his beliefs were based on reality. God knew exactly how Joseph was wired and what he was capable of. Joseph did not indulge himself or pity himself or take things into his own hands. He tethered himself directly to God, his Creator and Lord. Joseph's foundation was based on his relationship to God. Joseph knew that God created him and loved him, so there was no need to do anything to prove his worth. Joseph had no one to impress and no reason to pretend he was someone he was not. Why should he? The Creator of the universe already loved him. What more could he need? Joseph had incredible patience and never short-circuited his situation by taking matters into his own hands. Why would he need to? He was relying on God, and God's timing is always perfect. Joseph made excellent decisions because he utilized wisdom only God can give instead of basing things on his own human understanding. Joseph realized God's ways were better than his, so he abstained from the opportunity to commit adultery with Potiphar's wife, and he did not take revenge on his brothers when he had the chance. In the next several chapters, you will learn the incredible methods Joseph used, but please remember the importance of the foundation—of his belief system based on truth about himself and about God.[12]

Perhaps you are now questioning some of your paradigms. Maybe you've had some beliefs that have been negatively impacting your decision-making and attitude. How do you change that? What is the process for establishing a system of beliefs that is based on reality and real truth rather than on skewed perceptions?

We are inundated with information every second of every day. In today's society, with the advances of technology and media, we are exposed to more information than any generation in the past. There are thousands of voices calling out to us every day, and they are all saying something different. So which ones do you listen to? On what basis do you formulate your beliefs? What are you feeding your mind? The Bible says, "Do not conform any longer to the pattern of this world, but be transformed by the renewing of your mind. Then you will be able to test and approve what God's will is—his good, pleasing and perfect will."[13]

By now it should be clear that in order to create a climate for change, you first have to deal with your belief system.

I'm an average golfer, and I enjoy getting on the course from time to time. I have a basic understanding about the mechanics of a golf swing in terms of what to do and how to do it. When I'm feeling confident, I tend to hit the ball well. On one occasion, I was on the course with some friends, and I was playing what was, for me, a fantastic round. About halfway through the back nine, I suddenly fell apart. My entire game crashed and burned.

As I looked back on that round, I was able to dissect what went wrong. I had a bad drive on thirteen. My second shot was worse. And my mental state changed. Instead of thinking about making a great shot, I was focused on not screwing it up. My performance in the first half of the round was not in alignment with my real belief in myself as a golfer, because I had never played that well in the past. It was almost inevitable that I would self-destruct.

THE FIRST STEP IN CREATING A CLIMATE FOR CHANGE

The first step in creating a climate for change involves getting a baseline on your current beliefs (or paradigms), both good and bad. Once you start to understand what you believe about yourself and the world around you, you can then confirm whether those beliefs are valid or not. You might be operating under a set of beliefs that run contrary to reality, but if you aren't aware of those limiting beliefs, you'll try and try for change and never know why you are failing. As a result, your failure will ratify your incorrect paradigms.

At a very high level, you need to discover what you believe about God, the world, and yourself, and how all three of these interact. I encourage you to take a few moments of uninterrupted time to answer the questions below. These questions should initiate your process of understanding the paradigms that are limiting your potential. As you evaluate yourself, try your best to be objective and separate the truth from your feelings. As your awareness of your beliefs increases, your eyes will open to things you've never realized before.

- What are three beliefs that are limiting your life right now? What will your life be like ten and twenty years from now if you don't change these beliefs?
- What are your three greatest fears? Why do you think you have these three fears?
- Do you believe your actions are in line with your beliefs? Why or why not?
- Name one thing you wish you could be better at. Why?
- Name three things that you do extremely well. What tells you that you are good at these three things?
- What areas of your life are you confused about right now? Why are you confused?
- Do you believe in God? If no, why? If yes, do you believe you can know God?
- How do you see God and how do you see yourself in relationship to God?

THE SECOND STEP IN CREATING A CLIMATE FOR CHANGE

Once you've started the process of identifying your paradigms, the second step in creating a climate for change is asking yourself why and how you came to have each particular belief. Analyze the why and how questions of your paradigms.

In many cases, people form illogical beliefs based on an event that happened in their lives at some point in the past. When my dad was a boy, he and a friend enrolled in guitar lessons. He didn't last very long in his lessons, and years later, my dad always joked about the guitar teacher advising him to save his money and try something else. I heard this story many times when I was growing up, and I somehow linked in my head that my family did not have musical talent.

I always wanted to take guitar lessons, but I had this crazy belief that I was not capable of learning the guitar. I based this belief on my dad's self-deprecating humor. My parents never told me I couldn't play guitar, and they certainly would have supported the idea if I had expressed any interest. I did take some lessons when I was about ten years old, and I promptly quit when I realized it wasn't going to be easy. The initial difficulty of learning was validation to me that I did not have the talent to play.

Where did this belief come from? I came to an illogical conclusion and limiting belief through a poor interpretation of information. As a result, I spent many years wishing I could play without ever taking the steps to do so.

A few years later when I started college, I began to become aware of some of my limiting beliefs. I began to realize that my paradigm about my potential for guitar playing was probably not accurate, and so I took up the challenge once again. I pulled my old guitar out of the closet and found someone to start giving me lessons. A few years later, I was playing in blues, rock, and worship bands.

In many cases you will be quite surprised at how you came to believe what you believe about yourself and the world around you. If those beliefs are not in alignment with reality, then it will be like trying to find the courthouse in Chicago while using a map of Detroit. Your beliefs have more influence on your actions and potential than anything else.

Take an elephant as an example. When an elephant is born into captivity, its trainer will tie a rope around its leg and tie the other end of the rope to a stake. When the elephant is small, it doesn't have the strength to pull the stake from the ground. However, as it grows to full size, it has more than enough power to pull up the stake, but that never happens. Why? Because the elephant has a paradigm that says it's not possible based on its previous experience.

THE THIRD STEP IN CREATING A CLIMATE FOR CHANGE

The third step to creating a climate for change is identifying the difference between wanting to change and needing to change. You must have a strong and powerful desire for change, or otherwise you will be at the mercy of wishful thinking. Vince Lombardi once stated, "The difference between a successful person and others is not a lack of strength, not a lack of knowledge, but rather a lack of will."

If you are interested in making a change in your life, but you've struggled to follow through on making it happen, then you probably don't see the change as something that must happen. It's a nice-to-have, not a need-to-have. The difference is astronomical. Most college students need to improve their study habits.

At the beginning of the semester, improving study habits is simply a nice-to-have goal; that goal often changes to a need-to-have on the night before final exams when the difference between passing and failing is critical. Do you see the difference?

Change is almost impossible without fully understanding the need for the change. Wanting to change is not enough. You have to need it and need it bad. The problem for most people is that they have categorized the important need-to-have areas of their lives as nice-to-haves. So how do you create a burning desire for change by appropriately understanding the necessity and importance of change in your life?

In 1843, Charles Dickens wrote a book titled *A Christmas Carol*. The story follows a greedy and stingy businessman by the name of Ebenezer Scrooge. Scrooge has some paradigms that he's been living by for quite some time as a wealthy businessman. On the night of Christmas Eve, seven years after the death of his business partner, Jacob Marley, Scrooge is visited by three spirits—the Ghosts of Christmas Past, Present, and Future. The Ghost of Christmas Past takes him to a time in his life when he was happy and innocent. The Ghost of Christmas Present takes him to scenes he's never been aware of, including families in need. The Ghost of Christmas Future takes him to what his life will be like if he doesn't change his ways.

The process is a paradigm-altering experience for Scrooge because he starts to identify what's really important in his life. Charles Dickens's amazing story has been popular for the last hundred fifty years, and Dickens provides within it a process that can be used in your own life. This is a powerful process that involves analyzing your paradigms and playing them out to their logical conclusions. This process is so powerful that it has been used by motivational speakers like Tony Robbins as a means for affecting change.

Take a few moments and imagine that your own Ghost of Christmas Future is going to take you five years into the future. What does that look like if you stay on your current course? How will your paradigms and their resultant behaviors today affect the people in your life? How will they affect your relationship with your spouse, children, friends, coworkers, partners, God?

Once you've processed the idea of your paradigms played out in five years, imagine what your life will be like ten and then twenty years out. How does it feel? Can you live with the results? Are you willing to live with the results?

On January 15, 2009, United Flight 1549 crash-landed in the Hudson River after striking a flock of birds that took out both engines. Captain Chesley

Sullenburger was hailed as a hero after he successfully landed the plane on the Hudson. All one hundred fifty-five people on board survived. Coverage of the event was extensive, and I remember watching the interviews with Sullenburger and all the people aboard. As they were interviewed, people started to talk about their lives. Many stated that as a result of the crash landing and near-death experience, they realized they had a second chance at life. This was a great awakening for them personally. The idea of being so close to death jolted people into rethinking their lives and purpose.

I want you to know that you don't have to come within inches of losing your life in order to have a second chance. Your second chance starts right now. Take the time to evaluate your life and where it's headed. If this process is agonizing and difficult, then get excited. You will never change until you become disgusted, frustrated, and ready to transition from nice-to-have to need-to-have.

CHAPTER 3

Discovering Your True Voice

"You cannot consistently perform in a manner which is inconsistent with the way you see yourself."

ZIG ZIGLAR

One common thread among great entrepreneurs is an ability to be unique and to celebrate and promote that uniqueness. The great entrepreneurs usually find their success in an adventure that goes against the tide. They take the path less traveled and venture into uncharted waters against the waves of popular acceptance. They don't conform or succumb to peer pressure. Great entrepreneurs will take on new challenges and explore possibilities never thought possible by the general population. Most of the great products, services, and solutions that have changed and enhanced our world were creative and very different in their beginning.

What about you? Are you living in your uniqueness and loving every minute of it? Or perhaps your life is closer to that represented in the movie *The Matrix*, where life is simply a programmed distraction from reality and potential greatness.

I'll never forget when I finally decided I would take the leap into entrepreneurialism. The actual decision was almost ten years in the making as I agonized over the idea of taking the risk. Upon making the commitment to start a business, I was immediately faced with a monumental question. What was I going to do? What business would I start? It was a green field, and I could do virtually anything, but what?

That question instantly bred additional questions, like "What kind of entrepreneur will I be?" and "How will I be unique?"

Maybe you've asked similar questions about your life: Who am I? How am I unique? Who am I becoming? What's my purpose in life? Or perhaps you've never asked such questions because you're too distracted living the life of someone other than the authentic you.

Have you ever wanted to give up the façade of being someone you are not? Have you ever thought about just being the person God made you to be? What would it be like to just live without the encumbrances of another's opinions on your life's direction? John Eldredge writes in *Wild at Heart*, "I want to love with much more abandon and stop waiting for others to love me first. I want to hurl myself into a creative work worthy of God. I want to charge the fields at Bannockburn, follow Peter as he followed Christ out onto the sea, pray from my heart's true desire."[1]

The fact is that most people are pretending, living out a safe and acceptable life that is far from their true selves. I see it every day, especially in corporate America. There are many who are working hard to stay in the middle and never be noticed. Their *modus operandi* is that of flying under the radar by doing just enough to get by. They're on a homogenous, undercover mission for survival. Conform to the norms of society and do not stand out.

This pattern of behavior has become pervasive, but it's rarely recognized for what it truly is. In junior high, we identify it as succumbing to peer pressure, but in adult life, it's defined as being responsible and playing it safe. As we continue to conform by ignoring our true selves, we find ourselves acquiescing in every area of our lives. After a while, we don't know our own names. We've lost our identity, and we don't know where to go or what to do.

Gil Bailie once said, "Don't ask yourself what the world needs. Ask yourself what makes you come alive, and go do that, because what the world needs is people who have come alive." John Eldredge writes about this same idea in *Wild at Heart*:

All my life I had been asking the world to tell me what to do with myself. This is different from seeking counsel or advice; what I wanted was freedom from responsibility and especially freedom from risk. I wanted someone else to tell me who to be. Thank God it didn't work. The scripts they handed me I simply could not bring myself to play for very long. Like Saul's armor, they never fit. Can a world of posers tell you to do anything but pose yourself?[2]

Think about it for moment. Have you been asking the same questions? Are you looking for your true purpose? Are you living out life in complete fulfillment, or are you wearing a mask because you're too afraid to really be you?

Until you come to grips with your true identity, you will find yourself chasing the illusive idea of meaning and purpose only to discover you've been chasing the wrong thing upon capturing it. It's a vicious cycle that never ends. Most people never quite capture the definition of success they've created for themselves, so they continue living in a myth.

Stephen Covey states, "In more than 25 years of working with people… I have come in contact with many individuals who have achieved an incredible degree of outward success, but have found themselves struggling with an inner hunger, a deep need for personal congruency and effectiveness and for healthy, growing relationships with other people." Covey continues with a quote from a person he was personally working with, "I've set and met my career goals and I'm having tremendous professional success. But it's cost me my personal and family life. I don't know my wife and children anymore. I'm not even sure I know myself and what's really important to me. I've had to ask myself—is it worth it?"[3]

Gordon MacDonald writes in his book *Ordering your Private World*, "We must always be aware that there are leaders who can build great organizations (including churches) on natural gifts. Say the right words, be smart enough to do the right things, be insightful enough to connect with the right people, and one can go a long way before anyone ever discovers that the inner life is close to empty." MacDonald personally experienced this in his own life, and his book is a candid admission of his failure in life despite his outward success as a pastor and leader.[4]

Solomon, perhaps the wisest man to ever walk the earth aside from Jesus Christ, commented on his outward success:

I amassed silver and gold for myself, and the treasure of kings and provinces. I acquired men and women singers, and a harem as well—the delights of the heart of man. I became greater by far than anyone in Jerusalem before me. In all this my wisdom stayed with me. I denied myself nothing my eyes desired; I refused my heart no pleasure. My heart took delight in all my work, and this was the reward for all my labor. Yet when I surveyed all that my hands had done and what I had toiled to achieve, everything was meaningless, a chasing after the wind; nothing was gained under the sun.[5]

Tom Brady, the all-star football quarterback for the New England Patriots, has played in four Super Bowls and won three of them. He's won two Super Bowl

MVPs and played in five Pro Bowls, and he holds numerous records, including most touchdown passes in a single season, longest consecutive-win streak in NFL history, highest single-game completion percentage, most completions in Super Bowl history, and NFL MVP for 2007. Brady is well-liked, good-looking, and extremely wealthy. He has been known to date supermodels, and he's obviously one of the greatest quarterbacks in football history. In today's culture, can you imagine anything else this man needs?

Here's what Brady once said in an interview:

Why do I have three Super Bowl rings, and still think there's something greater out there for me? I mean, maybe a lot of people would say, "Hey man, this is what is." I reached my goal, my dream, my life. Me, I think, God, it's got to be more than this. I mean this can't be what it's all cracked up to be.[6]

For many who have not achieved the level of outward success they expect, there is great danger, because they have fooled themselves into believing their purpose is linked to future success. This hallowed belief will keep them chasing a lie for perhaps a lifetime. They say things to themselves like, "When I'm married, I'll be fulfilled. When I'm making six figures, I'll be satisfied. After I become a parent, I'll experience meaning. Once I get the promotion, drive the BMW, buy the big house, finish the degree, find acceptance with the right people..." and on it goes.

THREE FORCES THAT WILL BLIND YOU FROM YOUR TRUE SELF

There are several forces that will blind you from finding your true self and authentic fulfillment.

The first is that people who lack purpose don't know their names or who they are. Imagine what it would be like to have amnesia. You wake up tomorrow morning in a bed that is unknown to you. You don't recognize the people living with you. You have no idea what city or state or country you are in. You don't know what kind of person you are. You don't know who to trust or what to believe. What is your next step? Where do you go, and to whom do you go? The logical next step is that you have to find out who you are. You must discover your name.

In the movie *Gladiator,* the hero, Maximus, has gone from being the great commander of the Roman army to a gladiator with no identity. He ends up in this position because of the bloodthirsty scheming of Commodus, the emperor's son, who kills his own father and orders the execution of Maximus along with his wife and son. Later in the movie, Commodus approaches Maximus and asks him who he is. Commodus has no idea that the famous gladiator he is speaking to is the man he tried to kill. Maximus answers, "My name is Maximus Decimus Meridius; commander of the armies of the north; general of the Felix Legions; loyal servant to the true emperor, Marcus Aurelius; father to a murdered son; husband to a murdered wife; and I will have my vengeance, in this life or in the next."

Is there any question that Maximus knows who he is and what his name is? I once asked a small group I lead to share their favorite lines from a movie. One man answered with the above quote. John Eldredge writes about this same scene in *Wild at Heart*. This particular scene is so magnetic because it awakens a question in each one of us. What is my name? Who am I, and what am I to do?

The second force that blinds us from knowing our true selves is the fear of being different. This usually starts early in life when conforming appears to be the only socially acceptable approach. We don't want to stand out in the crowd. We don't want to be noticed. We don't want people to think we are different. In an effort to blend in with everyone else, we lose the very essence of our uniqueness. The qualities that represent our value and potential for greatness are squelched and hidden for fear of being different. This mindset and behavior becomes pervasive in your life when you begin to place importance of others' opinions above everything else. In an effort to seem acceptable to others, you forfeit your true identity in the process. As a result, you become a slave to those around you.

The fact is that people will place their own expectations on you, and you will be faced with a choice. Will you do what pleases those around you, or will you do what pleases God? God created you to serve him. Whenever you are serving God with your life, you are living as your "true self." When your actions are dictated by the opinions of others, you are missing the authentic life you were designed for.

The Bible says, "Am I now trying to win the approval of men, or of God? Or am I trying to please men? If I were still trying to please men, I would not be a servant of Christ."[7] Notice that the Bible states that if you are trying to please men, you cannot be a servant of Christ. At first glance, it's difficult to see the connection between pleasing someone and being a servant, but the point is that if you are trying to please someone, you are essentially acting as their servant. In an effort to blend in and not be different, you end up becoming a servant to those around you and thus becoming blind to your true self.

The third force hindering your true identity is the process of wishing you were something you are not. Have you ever wished you were more like a friend or someone else you know? Have you ever wanted to have the gifts, talents, or abilities of other people? The process of wishing to be someone different can have a devastating effect on you. In essence, you are telling God that you aren't happy with his work. You are ignoring the amazing abilities that you do have by focusing on the things that you don't have, resulting in a debilitating mindset.

Wishing for talents and abilities that you don't have can become one of the greatest stealth distractions in your life. This mindset is grounded in a self-indulgence that runs contrary to your true value. It can manifest itself in a competitive and ultimately destructive way, and it can be a drain on your self-esteem.

Discovering Your True Purpose

Once you've decided it is essential to discover your true self and purpose, you have to be willing to go to the source for the answers to your questions. As John Eldredge so eloquently put it, you can't go to a world of posers to learn anything besides how to pose.

Several years ago, Angie's grandfather passed away, and I inherited several of his tools. He was a woodworker and had a collection of very unique tools, but I had no idea what some of them were used for. One of those tools was an interesting little saw. I would occasionally use the saw to cut something, but it never did a really good job. I sometimes wondered what the saw was really designed for. I knew it probably had a special purpose, but I was oblivious to that purpose. At one point, I almost tossed the saw because I didn't see a need for it.

A few years later we decided to refinish all the floors in our home, and I started replacing the floor trim. One night a good friend who is a trained carpenter came over to help me out. I was struggling to make really good joints with the floor trim, and he told me I needed a cope saw. I didn't know if I had one, but we made a trip to my toolbox just to see. Sure enough, that seemingly useless little saw that I'd had for years was exactly what he was looking for! Within a few minutes, my friend taught me how to make flawless joints with this little saw. That saw went from being seemingly useless to being an indispensable tool with incredible value.

What made the difference? I discovered its purpose. My friend had insight into the design of that saw because he worked in the industry. What if you could have insight into the design of you? How would it be possible to access that type of information? The only way to ever tap into that information is to go to the source.

God created you and formed you before you were ever a twinkle in your parents' eyes. The Bible says:

> O LORD, you have searched me and you know me. You know when I sit and when I rise; you perceive my thoughts from afar. You discern my going out and my lying down; you are familiar with all my ways. Before a word is on my tongue you know it completely, O LORD. You hem me in—behind and before; you have laid your hand upon me. Such knowledge is too wonderful for me, too lofty for me to attain. Where can I go from your Spirit? Where can I flee from your presence? If I go up to the heavens, you are there; if I make my bed in the depths, you are there. If I rise on the wings of the dawn, if I settle on the far side of the sea, even there your hand will guide me, your right hand will hold me fast. If I say, "Surely the darkness will hide me and the light become night around me," even the darkness will not be dark to you; the night will shine like the day, for darkness is as light to you. For you created my inmost being; you knit me together in my mother's womb. I praise you because I am fearfully and wonderfully made; your works are wonderful, I know that full well. My frame was not hidden from you when I was made in the secret place. When I was woven together in the depths of the earth, your eyes saw my unformed body. All the days ordained for me were written in your book before one of them came to be.[8]

I want you to stop and go back and read that passage again. I believe its contents are so profound that it's virtually impossible to read it once and catch the majority of its meaning.

If God created you, and if you were fearfully and wonderfully made, then God has very specific information about you and your true purpose. He knows your name, and he knows what will make you completely fulfilled. You're utterly lost without him. C.S. Lewis once stated, "Until you have given yourself to him [God] you will not have a real self."

So, what does it mean to give yourself to God? It has more to do with relationship than it does with rules and procedures. If you invite Jesus Christ into your heart for your salvation and as the lord of your life, you are entering into relationship with him.

My son, Will, loves to play soccer. Soccer is the one sport I do know something about. I have played it my entire life and coached for years. One day he was trying to learn a move he'd seen on television. I knew the move quite well, so I proceeded to teach him how to do it. He quickly chastised me for interrupting him, firmly believing I had no idea how to do this move. I sat back and watched him for what seemed an eternity as he struggled to master it. Finally, in desperation, he looked to me and said, "Dad, can you please show it to me?" I just grinned and took the ball. Within a few minutes, I taught him the move. It was a joy to watch the amazement on his face and to see the building of trust in his heart. Maybe old Dad did know something after all.

We do the same thing with God. We struggle on our own to do something, and we believe we know best. We keep God on the sidelines, because we know better. God longs to show you his purpose. He's waiting on the sidelines for you to ask him, but he will not force himself on you. As you establish a relationship of trust and belief that God does know best, your true purpose will begin to actualize. It's an amazing process that can never be fully explained, only experienced firsthand.

The amazing discovery that you will make as you enter into a relationship with God is the plans he has for you. Imagine for a moment what you think those plans might be. I guarantee you his plans will greatly exceed your expectations! Your paradigm of who you are and what your purpose is will get turned on its head. Instead of striving to become someone you can never be, you will start to become exactly who God designed you to be.

Gary W. Chapman wrote a song that impacted me in an enormous way. I believe it accurately summarizes how we should think about our self-image. The song title is "All I Ever Have To Be," and the lyrics are:

When the weight of all my dreams
Is resting heavy on my head,
And the thoughtful words of health and hope
Have all been nicely said.
But I'm still hurting,
Wondering if I'll ever be
The one I think I am.
I think I am.
Then you gently re-remind me
That you've made me from the first,

And the more I try to be the best
The more I get the worst.
And I realize the good in me,
Is only there because of who you are.
Who you are...
And all I ever have to be
Is what you've made me.
Any more or less would be a step
Out of your plan.
As you daily recreate me,
Help me always keep in mind
That I only have to do
What I can find.
And all I ever have to be
All I have to be
All I ever have to be
Is what you've made me.[9]

I find incredible peace in the idea that all I ever have to be is what God created me to be. I don't have to do anything more than that. The pressures of the world and society can roll off my back like rain off a rooftop when my focus is set on God.

THE BENEFITS OF LIVING OUT OF YOUR TRUE PURPOSE

My sons, Wyatt, Will, and Peyton, and I have all been training under a senior black-belt instructor, Roy Hobbs. Sensei Roy is an amazing instructor, and he emphasizes the importance of proper technique. We learned early on in karate lessons that if you are performing a move incorrectly, you are wasting energy and simultaneously reducing the power of the blow. When your movements start to align with proper technique, your effectiveness increases exponentially and the energy required to perform the move is minimized.

It works the same way in our relationship with God. As you become aligned with God's plans for your life, you will be energized, not exhausted. I don't mean to say you will not work hard or that things will be easy, but you will derive energy and renewal as you live in alignment with your purpose. Your effectiveness, fulfillment, and sense of worth will be extremely high.

Once you start down the path of living in relationship with God, you will take on a confidence you've never experienced before. It will be a confidence completely grounded in God. When you live in confidence based on God's design and plans for you, you are no longer the slave to an unattainable life. You no longer play the part of the politician who strategically parses words so as not to lose favor with those around you while never really knowing who you are.

Eldredge states in *Wild at Heart,* "Let people feel the weight of who you are, and let them deal with it."[10] Those words blew me away the first time I read them. I had to analyze who I was seeking to please in my life. Was God my primary focus, or was I more concerned with what other people thought of me? Choosing to live exactly as God made you and then letting the people around you deal with it is the most freeing way to live. I have found that a person whose confidence is solely in God can be more persuasive simply with his or her actions than the most talented debaters in the world.

Once you've started down the path of authentic self-discovery, you will find it is easy to have passion in your life. The great entrepreneurs seem to exude passion. It is amazing how infectious a person of passion can be. I've witnessed entrepreneurs who have been passionate about things I initially found quite boring, but I found myself getting excited after seeing their passion. An entrepreneur will never find success with a new product or service if he cannot find and demonstrate passion to others, and you will struggle to find success without passion for the important things.

Genuine passion will come in your life when you are acting in congruence with your true purpose. I encourage you to become passionate about the important things of your life. It's time to get excited and charged up over the things that matter. Authentic passion will come alive in you when you start becoming exactly who God made you to be. You will light a wildfire of motivation when you start behaving in alignment with your true self. Why? Because God designed you with certain attributes, abilities, gifts, and interests. When you start exercising those areas in your life, it will be the equivalent of lighting the fuse on a rocket.

Have you ever met someone who lacked passion? A person lacking passion can literally suck the air right out of a room. I would rather watch paint dry than be stuck in a conversation with a person of no passion. On the other hand, a person who's passionate about the right things has the ability to inspire, motivate, and influence. Which would you rather be?

You can make an enormous impact in every area of your life when you start to live with passion. You will also make a positive impact in the lives of those around you. Do you struggle to get others excited and motivated? Are you interested in influencing your children in a positive way, but they just don't seem to listen? Are you going unnoticed at work or home? Do you struggle to motivate yourself? Authentic passion in the important areas of your life can turn the tide in a powerful way.

USING YOUR UNIQUENESS AS AN ADVANTAGE

As you discover God's blueprint for your life, you'll be amazed at how unique and amazing you are. Many people cringe at the idea of being unique, but you should embrace your uniqueness and celebrate it. You are not like any other person in the world! Every fingerprint is unique, and there is not a single duplicate. A large portion of your value is tied to your uniqueness and the way God created you.

It can become easy to compare your talents, abilities, and gifts with other people and falsely believe that you come up short. The truth is, your very "shortcomings" may be the things that propel you to greatness. Helen Keller, for example, became blind and deaf when she was only eighteen months old. She was unable to communicate or do virtually anything prior to meeting her mentor, Anne Sullivan. Despite these unbelievable setbacks, Helen Keller became a famous author and speaker. She met every US president from Grover Cleveland to Lyndon Johnson, and in 1964 she was awarded the Presidential Medal of Freedom, one of the United States's highest civilian honors.[11]

For almost a century, the Gracie family has been known for teaching and successfully competing in jiujitsu. Helio Gracie had four brothers who were all instructors, but Helio was extremely small and frail. His doctor recommended that he not participate in martial arts, and so he spent many years watching his brothers. Over time, Helio started to develop new techniques by modifying existing jiujitsu techniques to accommodate his fragile body. Helio did not have the strength or speed to execute the traditional jiujitsu moves that his brothers were teaching. Instead, Helio developed techniques and moves that emphasized leverage and timing so that even he could perform them.

Helio eventually became a world-famous fighter and purveyor of Brazilian jiujitsu. His adaptations became a game-changer in martial arts circles.[12] As a young man, he certainly could have been asking why he wasn't born stronger and faster, but instead, he used his uniqueness and changed everything. Would Helio ever have developed a modified jiujitsu approach if he had the same strength and speed as his brothers? Would Helen Keller ever have been a shining example of how to triumph in the face of adversity if she had not been blind and deaf?

Sometimes we see our uniqueness as negative because we don't see the entire picture. God has the perfect vantage point. He sees the entire picture, and he is our Creator. I assure you that you have gifts, talents, and potential for amazing, great things, even if those things are not visible to you now. Start the process of embracing who you are. You are unique and different from anyone else in the world, and you ought to be excited because of it.

The great entrepreneurs who have achieved extraordinary success have in most cases provided a product or service that was different. They have recognized and embraced a unique concept and developed it into something great. Thomas Edison brought some amazing, unique concepts to fruition, and they are now part of the fabric of modern culture. Edison invented the motion picture camera, the phonograph, the lightbulb, the stock ticker, a mechanical vote recorder, electrical power, a battery for an electric car, and thousands of other inventions. Modern mass communication is thanks to the direct influence of Edison.

Can you imagine what the world would be like today if Edison had tried to be like everyone else? It's interesting to note that Edison struggled in school as a child. He only attended school for about three months, and his teacher called him "addled," which means mentally confused. Edison also suffered from hearing impairment at a young age. Edison was homeschooled by his mother, and he said this of her: "My mother was the making of me. She was so true, so sure of me; and I felt I had something to live for, someone I must not disappoint."[13] Now ponder this question for a moment: what exactly did Edison's mother do for him? In addition to being a great mother, she caused Edison to discover who he already was. Edison was exactly as God made him.

I want you to know that you are exactly who God made you to be, even if you don't have someone like Thomas Edison's mother to tell you so.

YOUR PURPOSE IS GREATER THAN YOU

As you start to discover your true voice, I want to make one final, important point. Rick Warren wrote in *The Purpose-Driven Life*:

It's not about you. The purpose of your life is far greater than your own personal fulfillment, your peace of mind, or even your happiness. It's far greater than your family, your career, or even your wildest dreams and ambitions. If you want to know why you were placed on this planet, you must begin with God. You were born by his purpose and for his purpose.[14]

I know that most people do not want to hear that life is not all about them. Those words sting a bit, but they are true. Most self-help material that has been written, especially in the last several decades, is focused on you, you, and you. But you can never discover your true purpose and your true name without God. The Bible says, "It's in Christ that we find out who we are and what we are living for. Long before we first heard of Christ and got our hopes up, he had his eye on us, had designs on us for glorious living, part of the overall purpose he is working out in everything and everyone."[15]

Rick Warren goes on to state:

God has not left us in the dark to wonder and guess. He has clearly revealed his five purposes for our lives through the Bible. It is our Owner's Manual, explaining why we are alive, how life works, what to avoid, and what to expect in the future. It explains what no self-help or philosophy book could know…God is not just the starting point of your life; he is the source of it. To discover your purpose in life you must turn to God's Word, not the world's wisdom.[16]

God's game plan and purpose for your life is perfect, but you can't begin to move forward until you understand that game plan. Many times in my own life, I have liked to think that I was the one creating the game plan, and I just needed God to support it. That is futile and dangerous thinking. I can't begin to explain the incredible weight that will lift from your shoulders when you start to realize that life is not all about you. As your focus moves from self to God, your true purpose and value will come into view, and it will practically blind you it will be so obvious!

It is important to understand that your purpose cannot be understood through the development of a game plan and vision *first*. You have to know who you are and whom you serve first. You will either serve yourself, others, or God. As your focus shifts from self to God, your vision will become clear.

Jim Collins, author of *Good to Great,* defines a stark difference between the leaders of companies that made the leap to greatness in comparison to those that didn't. The great companies assembled the right team first, and then they defined the vision. The mediocre companies defined the vision first, and then they found a team to implement the vision.[17] I believe the difference has parallels to your own life, and the results can be profound. Once you know who you are and what your purpose is, then your vision and game plan will become visible.

In the chapters ahead, you will become equipped to make significant changes in your life. You will learn to take the amazing attributes of great entrepreneurs and apply them in your personal life. Remember that the following principles will only be techniques without a true and solid foundation. As you align your life with God's blueprint and purposes, your entire world will literally transform. It will be an exciting and adventurous process.

CHAPTER 4

Fear

"Courage emerges, not from increased police security, but from enhanced
spiritual maturity."

MAX LUCADO

When I was in junior high, my family and I traveled to Cincinnati, Ohio, for a soccer tournament. At the end of the tournament I was invited by one of my friends on the team to spend the weekend with his family at King's Island, a large amusement park. I was very excited, but I had one small problem: I was afraid of heights, especially tall roller coasters. I had never been able to muster the courage to "man up" and ride a roller coaster. I failed to mention this fear to my friend, Albert, and his mom and dad, who happened to love riding roller coasters.

I'll never forget the first few minutes in the park. Albert and his parents couldn't wait to hit the big coasters, and I was finally forced to confess my fear. You can imagine their disappointment. We went from ride to ride as I watched from the side in embarrassment. They each begged me to face my fear and take the plunge, but I wouldn't budge. I was terrified. I couldn't imagine being strapped in without the option of bailing if I changed my mind. I wanted so badly to have the courage, but I just couldn't talk myself into it.

After several hours of what was shaping up to be one of the worst days of my life, we came to a ride called "The Beast." The Beast opened in 1979 and was one of the longest, fastest, and tallest roller coasters in the world, and it is still considered the longest wooden coaster in the world today.[1] The name alone accurately describes this ride.

Throughout the day as we got into line for the different rides, I would also stand in line and then simply walk through when we reached the coaster. As we waited for the Beast, Albert's mom made a silent decision. She was going to make sure that I rode the Beast. When it finally became our turn to board the ride, Albert's mom jumped in front of me and would not let me pass through. I was stuck. At first I thought she was kidding, but then I realized she was not playing games.

I was now faced with a dilemma. I could turn back and fight through a crowd of thousands of people in complete humiliation, or I could sit down and buckle up. Just then, one of the attendants pushed me down in the seat and pulled the bar over my legs. I quickly buckled up. There was no turning back now.

Immediately the Beast began making its climb to the top of its first hill at one hundred and ten feet. This gave me plenty of time to reflect on the enormous mistake I had just made by getting on. I would have given anything to get off that ride!

Eventually we reached the top of the first hill, and I could see the entire breathtaking, intimidating layout of the ride. As the coaster crested the top, we began our plunge down one hundred and thirty-five feet into a covered tunnel. We were screaming at the top of our lungs, and I felt my stomach pulling a couple g's as my knuckles turned white from my death grip on the safety bar. As the coaster came out of the tunnel, it made a hard left-hand turn, and we felt the sensation of flying as we achieved hang time over the second hill. At that very moment, I realized something amazing. I was having the time of my life!

I instantly recognized that my fear, manifesting itself as anxiety, worry, and concern, had been robbing me of a great pleasure. For years I had avoided roller coasters and big theme parks, and it was all for nothing. It's ironic, because to this day, Angie and I are both big roller coaster junkies. We frequent some of the biggest parks in the country. I love the thrill and adrenaline rush that accompanies a ride on a big coaster.

Fear can be a powerful force. Zig Ziglar once defined fear as an acrostic that represents "False Evidence Appearing Real."[2]

Every entrepreneur who ventures out on his or her first project has dealt with some level of fear, and the great entrepreneurs have learned how to effectively manage their fear and use it to their advantage. I learned early on as an entrepreneur that hidden fears can keep you out of the game and on the sidelines. In the pages that follow, we are going to address fear from several perspectives. While my fear of roller coasters was illogical and baseless, there are fears you may struggle with every day that are rooted in experience—perhaps your own personal experience. We will explore the many facets of fear, and you will discover a process for determining good fear from bad and how to manage fear and effectively use it to your advantage.

Before we address the negative components of fear, I want you to know that fear can serve as a great protector. When I was sixteen years old, I used to drive a 1979 black Trans Am with a four-hundred-cubic-inch engine and a four-speed manual transmission. I drove that car at speeds beyond one hundred thirty mph with no thought of ever being in accident. It is a miracle that I am alive today. The truth is that I had no fear of being harmed when I drove that car because I was young and not very smart. Through the years, I lost a few friends to car accidents, and I was also involved in a few accidents myself. As a result, I now have a very healthy fear of what an automobile can do if it is not driven with care and attention.

I now drive our family minivan (notice I am not sharing engine size or other performance-related information with you) with my wife and children at speeds under the speed limit. I am a very safe and responsible driver because I have a healthy fear of what can happen.

Fear can protect us and serve as a great guide before we are about to do something dangerous. In the Bible, we learn that the beginning of wisdom is the fear of the Lord. The word "fear" in the verses that state this is used to denote respect or reverence. This is a healthy aspect of fear.

Healthy fear has its benefits, but it is imperative that you understand the line between healthy fear and destructive fear. A simple and quick way to determine the difference is to identify the consequences of a particular fear in your life. Employ the Scrooge method again. If the consequences are constructive and positive, and they are not limiting your potential or ability, then your fear is probably healthy. My safe driving is a good example of this. But what if my fear of automobile safety resulted in me avoiding driving altogether? What if I chose never to leave my home for fear of being in an accident? In that case, my fear would have crossed the line to an unhealthy level.

Going forward, we are going to address the type of fear that is paralyzing and destructive. We are going to analyze three types of fear that will stop you in your tracks and render you useless. You will also learn some incredible strategies for how to address and control your fears, and you will learn how to take fear and use it to your advantage.

Many people are suffering from fear in their lives because of past experiences. They have witnessed and lived through terrible situations. You might be struggling right now with a very real fear in your life. Perhaps you were hurt by someone in the past, or you may have lost someone close to you. All these things can affect how you look at the present and future.

On January 28, 1986, the space shuttle *Challenger* disintegrated just seventy-three seconds into its flight. The entire world was horrified as footage of the disaster aired live on television. NASA lost its entire crew of seven, including Christa McAuliffe, the first member of the Teacher in Space Project. It was a tragedy that many will never forget. The shuttle program was grounded for almost three years due to the accident.

On the morning of September 29, 1988, the space shuttle program would re-emerge as the space shuttle *Discovery* was poised to lift off. It would be the first shuttle flight since the *Challenger* disaster. Can you imagine what was going through the minds of the crew and their families on the morning of that launch? Do you think they were struggling with some level of fear? It would certainly not be unfounded! Fear is an emotional state of distress brought on by imminent danger, whether real or imagined.

You may have some legitimate fears you are struggling with, but you must determine if those fears are beneficial or harmful. Is your fear hindering your ability to live as you ought to be living? It's important to note that the space shuttle program returned to space. Fear was present in the minds of the crew, NASA staff, and families on the morning of January 28, 1986, but don't forget that the shuttle launched. Fear did not prevent the shuttle crew from moving forward.

Unhealthy fear can have devastating effects on your life and well-being, and it can drive you to worry about things you cannot control. Unhealthy fear can leave you with a feeling of helplessness and vulnerability, and it will keep you from taking action. Fear can consume your entire thought process and paralyze you. In essence, fear that is unchecked will maintain a death grip on you.

Hidden Unhealthy Fears

As your understanding of fear expands, it's important to note that hidden fears can do the most damage in your life, because you haven't recognized their control and impact on you. You may not be aware of a particular fear that is hindering you from taking action or is causing you a great deal of anxiety and concern. We will explore three unhealthy fears that you may be struggling with without realizing it.

The first unhealthy fear is the no-confidence fear. This fear is prevalent in those who don't believe they can come through when needed. They don't believe in themselves, and they choose to avoid taking on challenges, goals, and tasks because they fear that if they fail, their failure will validate a hidden belief that they do not have value. A person with the no-confidence fear will never step up and lead. Such people fear that their inadequacies will be discovered, and so they avoid risk at all cost. People who struggle with this fear are usually very good at making excuses.

I have a friend who is extremely intelligent, but he struggled a great deal in college. One of the biggest reasons for his struggles in school was his failure to attend classes on a regular basis. I recall one semester when my friend had recommitted himself to working hard in school. He decided that he would work hard in a particular class that semester. But after his first exam in the class, he quit attending.

I remember asking him why he had given up so quickly. I learned that he had received a B- on his first exam. He shared with me that if it wasn't possible to achieve an A in the class, then he didn't want to continue trying. I think his response revealed a lot about his struggles in college.

My friend suffered from the no-confidence fear. In his own mind, he could always justify his poor grades by his lack of attendance. But how could he ever justify poor grades if he showed up on a regular basis and tried as hard as he could? What then if he failed?

Do you see what he was doing to himself? He was too afraid to really try, because deep down, he didn't think he was enough. It was much easier for him to create an excuse for himself than to deal with the reality that he might fail. This type of fear will cause a person to play defense, and in a worst-case scenario, to practice self-sabotage.

You may find yourself constantly unwilling to step out to take a risk or challenge, and you may not even know why. In situations where you start to experience success, you may even start looking for opportunities to sabotage your own success, because in a subconscious way, you don't believe you can pull it off. Deep down, you may believe that you are doomed to failure, so you may as well help that process along rather than wait out the inevitable. You may hold to this paradigm without even realizing it.

I urge you to do some self-reflection and consider whether you are struggling with this fear. You may long for the opportunity to really step up and take on the world by taking calculated risks and challenges. You may dream of accomplishing great achievements in your life, and yet you have never taken even a small step in that direction. If you haven't, then stop now and ask yourself why. Is there one thing that you wish you were doing in your life right now, but you aren't taking action? Think about this situation and analyze why. Your first response will probably include a lot of excuses that will serve as a cover for the real, underlying reason you have not taken action. It's time to take a hard look in the mirror and ask the tough questions.

The second unhealthy fear is the peer-approval fear. This fear is driven by a desire for the approval of others, and in many cases, of one particular person, such as a parent, spouse, friend, or boss. The person who struggles with the peer-approval fear is attempting to validate his or her self-worth through the opinions of others. These people will never take action because they're so consumed with what others will think. I'll give a personal example to demonstrate.

I had the great fortune and God's wonderful blessing to marry my high-school sweetheart. I was blessed with the opportunity to marry up, and I have experienced great blessings in my marriage to Angie. Over the years, I have come to care greatly about what Angie thinks of me. I've adopted this paradigm in a subconscious way.

Angie is a great encourager, and she is extremely supportive. She has one of the most positive personalities of anyone I've ever met. She can be in a devastating circumstance and still maintain a positive attitude and outlook. I've had the good fortune to achieve some marginal successes, and I owe a large part of the credit to Angie and her encouragement.

Early in our marriage and in our dating years, Angie encouraged and supported me through some good successes. During this same time, I wanted to start my own business and become a successful entrepreneur. I cannot even begin to explain how badly I wanted to own a business. I dreamed about it and talked about it and agonized over how to do it. I read hundreds of books and considered all kinds of opportunities. I just could never find the right one. I needed a fail-proof opportunity before I would be willing to take such a risk. (For those of you who have lived a while, can you think of any challenge that is fail-proof?) Time was not on my side, because Angie and I started having children. Our first son, Wyatt, came along, and then our second son, Will, was born. And then Angie became pregnant with our third son, Peyton. I was getting older and more risk averse, and I still had no plans for a business that I could start or own.

Can you guess why I was still on the sidelines and not in the game of owning my own business? Yes: I was afraid. I feared letting my wife down. What if I started a business and it failed? My wife would look at me as a failure, and I would be humiliated and embarrassed. I also had children who would one day grow up and learn that their father was a failure. I was thinking these very thoughts, and yet I was not consciously aware of them. I just told myself that I couldn't find the right business.

I complained to Angie on a regular basis that I just couldn't find the right business. The real truth was that I had probably identified several viable business opportunities, but I was unwilling to risk being a failure in her eyes. Zig

Ziglar once said, "If you want to own your own business and you don't, it's because you are afraid."

Like me, you may be seeking the approval of someone who depends on you. You may be chasing the approval of someone who may never give it to you. You might be trying to gain the approval of a father or mother who isn't even alive today. Consider that God loves you, and that your value is not based on anything but that one fact. Your desire to find approval in the eyes of anyone other than God will almost always lead to a peer-approval fear. As a result, you'll never actualize the potential God gave you in his specific design of you.

The third unhealthy fear is the loss-of-control fear. When I travel, I prefer to drive instead of flying. I don't mind the idea of flying, but I do mind the idea of not being in control. It bothers me to be on a plane and have to trust in someone else to control that plane. I'm not even a pilot, and it bothers me! What's worse for me than flying? Riding in an automobile as a passenger. Why? Because I am not in control.

In the movie *Days of Thunder,* Cole Trickle describes what it's like to drive a race car: "Speed. To be able to control it. To know that I can control something that's out of control." Later in the movie, Cole's girlfriend, Dr. Claire Lewicki, replies, "Control is an illusion, you infantile egomaniac. Nobody knows what's gonna happen next: not on a freeway, not in an airplane, not inside our own bodies, and certainly not on a racetrack with forty other infantile egomaniacs."

The greatest problem with this fear is that control is an illusion. Most of the things you will never be able to control in your life are the very things you agonize over and fear. This fear, if it remains unchecked, can lead to a crippling state. It's related to fears of loss, helplessness, the unknown, death, lack of security, and so on. If you allow this fear to control you, you will struggle with anxiety, worry, and concern, and it will affect your attitudes and behavior. You will never be willing to take action, and your focus will always be on what could go wrong instead of what could be possible. I can speak from experience: this type of fear can be exhausting, mentally and emotionally.

I want you to take a few minutes and analyze what fears you might be struggling with in your life right now. If it's possible to break away without any distractions, please answer the following questions:

- What are your three greatest fears?
- For each of the three fears that you just listed, identify whether the fear falls into one of the three areas described earlier: no-confidence fear,

peer-approval fear, or loss-of-control fear.

- Once you've identified each of the three fears, ask yourself what caused you to adopt each of the three fears in your life.
- List the consequences (present and future) of these fears for you and those around you. What opportunities are you missing? What toll is your anxiety having on your peace of mind?
- Think of someone you know and trust to share your current fears with, and write down your fears to share with that person later. Documenting your fears and talking them through with someone you trust can help bring clarity.

As you go through the process of identifying your greatest fears and begin to understand the destructive consequences of those fears, you are going to be faced with a decision. Either you will face your fears directly and deal with them, or you will continue to pretend they do not exist. Only you can make that decision.

In *The Empire Strikes Back,* Luke Skywalker comes to a point in his Jedi training where he must face his fears. Yoda tells him to enter a cave. Luke says, "There's something not right here…I feel cold…death." He then asks Yoda, "What's in there?"

Yoda replies, "Only what you take with you." The Jedi Master continues, "Your weapons…you will not need them." Yet Luke takes his light saber with him, afraid to face the unknown without it. We'll come back to this story as we continue to discuss the concept of overcoming our fears.

OVERCOMING YOUR FEAR

Facing your fears can be daunting, but it is necessary. You must do it. The problem is that we don't know how things are going to turn out, and that is a scary proposition. That is why Luke was unwilling to leave his weapon when Yoda prompted him to. Luke didn't know how things were going to turn out.

Oswald Chambers writes in *My Utmost for His Highest:*

Naturally we are inclined to be so mathematical and calculating that we look upon uncertainty as a bad thing… To be certain of God means that we are uncertain in all our ways, we do not know what a day may bring forth. This is generally said with a sigh of sadness; it should rather be an expression of breathless expectation.[3]

John Eldredge writes in *Wild at Heart*, "The greatest obstacle to realizing our dreams is the false self's hatred of mystery. That's a problem, you see, because mystery is essential to adventure. More than that, mystery is the heart of the universe and the God who made it."[4]

Eldredge goes on to explain that everything important that a man will face in his life is filled with mystery, but we should not look at that as a bad thing. Eldredge explains that mystery should be viewed as an exciting and essential part of life and a key component to adventure.

I don't know about you, but I struggle with mystery. I don't like surprises, and I want to know exactly how things are going to turn out. There can be great anxiety in not knowing what will happen next. Our desire to be all-knowing will usually lead to fear, lack of adventure, and paralysis. So how do you face your fears? What is it that you must do?

First, understand that fear is something you will continually have to confront. So admit it when you are afraid. Denial only makes things worse. Imagine that you have cancer, but instead of facing the cancer directly, you choose to live in denial. That is a dangerous place! God encourages us throughout the Bible to not be afraid. He references fear and how to handle fear throughout Scripture, so it is acceptable to admit that you will struggle with fear from time to time. Awareness and admission is the first step to facing the fear.

Second, you must determine who God is and who you are in relation to him. If you are living under a paradigm that says you control everything and all things depend on you, then you have placed yourself in the position of God. Good luck with that! I know how it will turn out for you, because I've made that mistake before. Taking on the weight of the world is not an enjoyable experience. When everything depends on you and your own abilities, you will struggle to find confidence, you will worry about what others think of you, and you will manipulate and labor for control. You will never give yourself over to mystery. If it's not possible to know the exact outcome, you will never step up and live as God has planned. Your life will be marked with worry, anxiety, and fear.

John Eldredge writes about his own struggles in *Wild at Heart*:

Something in me felt young—like a ten-year-old boy in a man's world but without a man's ability to come through. There was much fear beneath the surface; fear that I would fail, fear that I would be found out, and finally, fear that I was ultimately on my own.[5]

I must admit I've struggled with those same feelings whenever I've placed myself on the throne of my life instead of placing God there.

My own fears increased quite a bit after I became a father. I found myself worrying about things beyond my control, and I questioned my own ability to come through as a father and protector of my family. I never felt that way as a boy when I lived under my father's protection. I never worried about anything, because I always knew my dad had it under control. But later, as a father and husband myself, I started to be consumed with the idea that I was in control and responsible for other lives.

It's true that I am responsible for my family, and there are several people who rely on me for leadership at one level or another. As responsibilities and pressures increase, so the level of fear and worry in our lives can also increase. There is certainly a strong correlation between the level of responsibility we have and the amount of fear and anxiety we struggle with, but the fear is caused by where we place our confidence. If your confidence rests solely in your own ability to come through, then you already know deep down that you are not an all-knowing, all-powerful god. This basic understanding will register in your brain, and so fear can take over.

A couple years ago my son, Will, had swollen lymph nodes. My father-in-law had recently passed away from cancer, so Angie and I were concerned. We took Will to the doctor, and they started doing some tests. I remember giving him a hug one night, and I wouldn't let go. He said, "Dad, you can stop hugging me now." I just remember thinking, "I am his father, and I have to protect him." But there was nothing I could do if he was really sick. I'm not God, and I can't really do anything. The same is true for you. If all your confidence is placed solely in yourself, then fear will take over.

There are many parents who deal with this situation every day. We were very fortunate because Will turned out to be fine, but there are millions of children who don't turn out fine. As a parent, how do you deal with that situation? Fear can literally take over and control you.

It is imperative that you understand the difference between you and God. You must rely on God, and nothing else, as your confidence.

At the end of Moses's life, a man named Joshua took over his position of leading Israel. Moses was an absolutely incredible leader and man of God. This was the guy who led the Israelites out of Egypt; he led the Israelites through the Red Sea that God literally parted before them; and he was given the Ten Commandments from God. That's quite a resume! Joshua was then called to take over and lead Israel into the Promised Land. Joshua's level of responsibility increased expo-nentially. He was now the man everyone was looking to. I can just imagine the pressure and anxiety that Joshua was taking on!

The Bible says:

> After the death of Moses the servant of the LORD, the LORD said to Joshua son of Nun, Moses' aide: "Moses my servant is dead. Now then, you and all these people, get ready to cross the Jordan River into the land I am about to give to them—to the Israelites. I will give you every place where you set your foot, as I promised Moses. Your territory will extend from the desert to Lebanon, and from the great river, the Euphrates—all the Hittite country—to the Great Sea on the west. No one will be able to stand up against you all the days of your life. As I was with Moses, so I will be with you; I will never leave you nor forsake you. Be strong and courageous, because you will lead these people to inherit the land I swore to their forefathers to give them. Be strong and very courageous. Be care-ful to obey all the law my servant Moses gave you; do not turn from it to the right or to the left, that you may be successful wherever you go. Do not let this Book of the Law depart from your mouth; meditate on it day and night, so that you may be careful to do everything written in it. Then you will be prosperous and successful. Have I not commanded you? Be strong and courageous. Do not be terrified; do not be discour-aged, for the LORD your God will be with you wherever you go.[6]

In this passage, God tells Joshua to be strong and courageous. He repeats that command, not just advice, repeatedly throughout these nine verses. God tells Joshua not to be terrified. God commands Joshua not to fear. Why does God repeatedly tell Joshua not to fear, and to be strong and courageous? Because God knew that Joshua was suffering with fear.

God usually attaches conditions to the promises that he makes to us. God told Joshua not to fear and to be strong and courageous, but he also put some conditions in place. God told Joshua to obey his commands. God even gave Joshua a road map for obedience. In order to be successful in obedience, Joshua needed to be in God's Word on a regular basis. God said to not let this book depart from his mouth, and he said to meditate on it day and night. And here's the really important part: God said, "Be careful to do everything written in it."

There is an amazing sense of peace that will accompany true allegiance to

God. I love the idea that God will be with me wherever I go. I want you to know that God made some incredible promises to Joshua, but Joshua still had to do the work. It wasn't as if God would go and face the giants while Joshua sat back and waited. No, Joshua had to step up to the plate and face down his fears, but Joshua's confidence was not in his own abilities. Joshua's confidence was placed in God. That is the great distinction.

God makes some amazing promises to you, but that is not a pass for you to avoid whatever it is that you now face or will face in the future. You will also have to step up to the plate and face down your own dark cave, your own giants. It has been said that courage is not an absence of fear. General George Patton once said, "All men are afraid in battle. The coward is the one who lets his fear overcome his sense of duty." Mark Twain said, "Courage is resistance to fear, mastery of fear, not absence of fear."

In my humble opinion, there is only one situation in which we should fear. We should be afraid when we are not at the center of God's will. If we are in God's will, there is never a time when we should succumb to fear. In fact, we should be strong and courageous. We should live as fearless men and women with great confidence and courage.

The Bible says, "Do not be anxious about anything, but in every situation, by prayer and petition, with thanksgiving, present your requests to God. And the peace of God, which transcends all understanding, will guard your hearts and your minds in Christ Jesus."[7] The Bible is clear that you shouldn't worry about anything as long as you are trusting in God. It even says that God will guard your heart and mind, and that his peace transcends all understanding. There are many things that we will never understand about God and certainly about our own circumstances. Yet God promises that he will provide peace despite the fact that we do not understand.

God will also guard your heart and your mind. The Bible says, "When calamity comes, the wicked are brought down, but even in death the righteous seek refuge in God."[8] God protects even in death. On the surface that may seem like a contradiction, but from God's vantage point, it makes perfect sense. There is no reason to fear, even death, if you are a child of God. God provides the prescription and the peace, but we are required to be in relationship with him.

The Bible says that Jesus is the Prince of Peace.[9] God doesn't just bring peace into your life. He is peace, the Prince of Peace. He is the very essence of peace, and peace cannot be attained outside of him. I'm not referring to a synthetic, artificial peace, but authentic peace that only God can provide.

One issue that many people struggle with is the idea of turning it over. When you place God at the center of your life, you are going to obey his commands and do things his way, not yours. When you put this into practice, you will be equipped with courage, peace, and the strength to face anything—but most people are not willing to let go. Luke Skywalker refused to leave his light saber behind at the urging of Yoda. Placing yourself in a humble position under God's provision means giving up control. The tighter you hold on, the higher your anxiety will go.

Max Lucado wrote in *Fearless: Imagine Your Life Without Fear,* "Courage emerges, not from increased police security, but from enhanced spiritual maturity."[10] I have learned that authentic courage should be based on my dependence on God and not on my own false sense of security or hyped-up self-delusion that I can handle it on my own. Courage follows faith. "Feed your fears, and your faith will starve. Feed your faith, and your fears will."[11]

Third, once you've placed God in the appropriate place in your life, recognize that courage is a muscle. It is not possible to simply eliminate fear from your life in one instant. It's much like exercise. You will need to practice courage on a consistent basis for the rest of your life, but it will get easier with practice. Several years ago I started running. At first I couldn't run more than a mile or two. Over time, with a lot of practice and exercise, I could run ten miles at one time. Courage is similar in that, as you exercise the muscle of courage, you will be able to practice it more consistently and effectively.

Using Fear as an Advantage

Once you've begun the process of dealing with your fears, you can start to use fear to your advantage. Entrepreneurialism is a process that almost inherently forces people to deal with their fears. When I quit my full-time job to start a technology company, I discovered a powerful principle which yielded amazing results. I deliberately put myself in a position of no turning back. At first, the very idea of being in such a position was my greatest fear! I was supporting a family of five with no additional income. By quitting my full-time job, I left us with no source of income. But it was this very position of no turning back that fueled my work ethic and resolve. My fear of not being able to support my family was much greater than my fear of calling new clients and giving my new business everything I had to give.

Putting yourself in a position of no turning back may terrify you, but the power of it can be a great motivator. Hernan Cortes put this same principle to work in his conquests in the early 1500s. Cortes and his men landed at Vera Cruz in an extremely difficult campaign. Cortes ordered that all of his own ships be destroyed when they first landed on the coast.[12] This very act put his small army in a no-turning-back position. It would be impossible to retreat, because their only means of escape was destroyed. It is amazing what people can accomplish when they can place their entire focus on the task at hand, without competing thoughts of retreat and giving up.

You can utilize the no-turning-back approach with accountability partners. Perhaps you are struggling to change some area of your life, but you are the only one aware of the struggle. Sharing this situation with someone you trust and know well can put you in a no-turning-back situation. Once you've committed to a change, you now have someone to keep you accountable. If you get off track, you will be forced to answer for it.

One area of fear that can hinder personal growth is that of being in uncomfortable situations. Most people avoid getting out of their comfort zones. As a result, our fears of being uncomfortable can prevent us from growing and maturing. For example, lifting weights requires that you take a muscle and make it feel very uncomfortable for a period of time. Yet, as you tear and stretch the muscle, it rebuilds as stronger and more effective.

Most people do not enjoy being uncomfortable, but benefit comes with enduring. The Bible says, "Consider it pure joy, my brothers, whenever you face trials of many kinds, because you know that the testing of your faith develops perseverance. Perseverance must finish its work so that you may be mature and complete, not lacking anything."[13]

It is hard to imagine, but problems create opportunity for growth and maturity. Think back now on any problem you've ever experienced in your life. Isn't it true that you learned something or grew stronger as a result of that problem? (If that is not the case, then I would argue that you have missed a great learning opportunity to truly see the experience for what it was. Perhaps it's time to see if you can use the opportunity to learn from it today.)

When I quit my full-time job to start the technology company, Angie was pregnant with our third child, and she was a stay-at-home mother. We had recently built a brand-new house and decided not to move into it in lieu of starting this new business. We had also recently sold a rental home that we owned in order to consolidate our finances. It was a risky venture because we did not have wealthy parents or a large savings in place as a safety net to fall back on if the business failed.

One month after quitting my job and starting this new company, it felt like the entire world started falling square on my head. Here's the short list of what happened next:

- My previous employer filed a lawsuit against me claiming that I was competing with them and in violation of my non-compete.
- The new owner of our previous rental home filed a lawsuit against us over an issue with the basement.
- Our neighborhood, where we had been living for seven years, was identified by the EPA as a lead-contaminated site from several years earlier, and our entire yard would have to be replaced.
- Our children and unborn child were at risk for lead poisoning during the remediation process.
- Angie started to have pregnancy complications and was placed on bed rest for the last three months of her pregnancy, and we still had two small children at home to be cared for every day.
- Our unborn child was found to have a two-strand umbilical cord, and the doctors were concerned our third child might be born with Down's syndrome.
- The new house we built was for sale for almost a year without a single offer, and we were carrying two house payments with no income.

I was trying to start a brand-new business from scratch, and it was the first time I had ever attempted such a venture. You could say I was feeling the pressure! I found it difficult to think about the future. One thing after another continued to happen, and I simply focused on one day at a time. I was working extremely hard and refused to give in, but I was longing for relief.

I don't remember smiling much during those tumultuous eight months. There are millions of people who have gone through much worse than I did, but it's hard to get perspective when you're the one in the storm. I was feeling very vulnerable and extremely fragile… but let me share what happened through that situation.

- I learned that I should never place faith in personal assets or things or health or money, because they can go away in a second without warning.
- I realized that I cannot control anything; only God is in control.

- I learned that God will never give you more than you can handle, and he will never leave you nor forsake you.
- I discovered the value in keeping an intimate relationship with God on a daily basis and not just when I needed help with a crisis.
- I learned that no matter what your circumstances are, you can find the positive.
- I discovered that problems will create perseverance if you choose to continue.
- I learned to never give up. No matter what, never give up!

I can assure you the lessons I learned from that entire experience have contributed significantly to the man I am today. You can't buy that kind of experience, and I learned to depend on God and God alone. Faith in anything else will leave you devastated and defeated. Consider it joy when you face trials, because the learning experience will change your entire life.

Approximately eight months after my trials started, I finally turned my anxiety and worry over to God. I acknowledged my lessons, and I simply trusted in God for the future. Not long after that, every issue listed above was resolved. I could breathe a sigh of relief, but I've never forgotten the valuable lessons I've learned.

Not all uncomfortable situations are as bad as the one I described above. Many times, I have imagined an unknown situation to be uncomfortable only to discover that it was simply my imagination getting the better of me. I've avoided several situations in the past based on an inaccurate paradigm. My fear was simply a figment of my own imagination. I now force myself to get uncomfortable every so often so that I don't fall into the habit of avoiding fear! I will sometimes attend an event where I don't know anyone just to put myself out of my comfort zone. The practice of facing small fears will provide a foundation for facing bigger fears in the future.

I can assure you that the process of addressing your fears is the most liberating and exciting practice you can imagine. You will be free to take on the challenges God created you for with peace and resolve. Imagine the new things you might discover about yourself and the world around you!

CHAPTER 5

Priorities

"We prioritize the things that only last for a moment, and we hardly notice the things that will last forever."

RICK WARREN

When I was a junior in high school, my family and I took a trip to a lake in Indiana for a week of waterskiing and fun. I brought a friend with me, and we took two cars. My parents and my brother were in one car, and my friend and I were in the other.

I'd only had my driver's license for about nine months, so I was not accustomed to reading maps and watching for landmarks. I just followed my dad all the way. When he exited for gas, I followed him. When it was time to stop and eat, I followed him to the restaurant. I didn't even know the name of the place we were going or the name of the lake or town we were heading to. I just knew it was a lake in Indiana.

When we were within an hour or so of our final destination, I lost my dad. One minute we were following him, and the next minute he was gone. My friend and I were probably having some deep conversation about music or cars or something that high-school boys tend to talk about, but somehow I found myself with no one to follow.

To compound the problem, we were now on a back road, off the main interstate. I felt like Lightning McQueen from the movie *Cars*. This was my status:

- I didn't know where we were.
- I had no idea where we were going.
- I didn't have a map (navigation systems had not been invented yet).
- There was no cell phone.
- I had never been in the area we were driving in.
- There were no gas stations or places of business in the immediate area.
- We had no game plan.

Have you ever been in that situation before? I didn't know if we should just pull over or keep driving or try to find some place to stop. It was total confusion. There was no way to communicate. Even if I stopped for directions, what would I say? "Can you help me get somewhere? I don't really know where it is, but I sure could use some help."

Millions of people are living out that situation every day in their personal lives. They started off by following someone, probably their parents or maybe their friends. There wasn't a need to really do much thinking or planning, because those things were done for them on a daily basis. Maybe they went to college, or perhaps they started a job out of high school. Maybe they never finished high school, or maybe they got one degree after another for years and years.

And then something happened. They realized they had no idea where they were, where they were going, or how to communicate. They had no game plan of any kind. When you don't have a target destination, what do you do? You can take action, but what action do you take?

Most people just try to do *something,* regardless of the result. Action makes us feel that we are in control. It gives us a false sense of accomplishment. The problem is that action without a plan is simply aimless busyness.

A majority of the thought leaders on goal setting and achievement today believe that over 97 percent of the people in the world have no written goals or plans for their lives.[1] If that is true, then most people have never thought through what is important in their lives.

REASONS WHY PEOPLE DO NOT HAVE A PLAN

When I first learned this, I had to ask the question, why? Why would so many people wander around with no definite plan or purpose? I believe there are several reasons.

First, people don't see the value in taking the effort or time to plan. If you don't see the value or importance of planning your life, then why take the time to go through the exercise?

Several years ago during the dot-com bubble of the late 1990s, I had a customer who wanted to build a web application for a new business he had started. This was during the time when companies were being started with venture capital on crazy ideas using the Internet as a platform for business. Countless companies were being formed every day in rapid succession. The Internet was exploding, and there was a mad dash among these new companies to capitalize on their respective markets. Billions of dollars were being pumped into them with no real business plans or strategies for how to make money.

Every company name ended with ".com," and it was being reported that a new economy was taking over. If you didn't get in on it, your old brick-and-mortar businesses would soon make you obsolete.

My customer was an extremely wealthy individual, and he wanted in on the dot-com game. He had a business idea and he had the money. At the time I was fascinated with what was happening in the market. I could never understand how these new companies were making any money. Later I came to learn that they *weren't* making money, and that's why most of them are out of business today. I remember asking this customer, "What's your business plan? What market research did you do to determine this was a viable business?"

He responded by stating that there was not enough time to do any market research. He also admitted, after some probing, that there was no business plan. He said that if he spent the time it would take to do research and develop a plan, the window of opportunity would be gone. He had limited time, and he had to launch the site as soon as possible. If a competitor got to the market first, his chances for success would be limited.

We started work immediately. We met all his milestones, and we kept the project under budget. My project manager and development team worked diligently, pulling seventy-hour workweeks to just make it. I'll never forget when we delivered the product. My customer had flown in that morning, and we met for lunch. He handed me the final check, and we turned over the code. He shared with me that the product would never be launched. He had spent in excess of two million dollars, including large amounts of time and effort, on a business that closed its doors before it ever opened.

By this time, start-up dot-com companies were going down in flames in droves as the new economy was evaporating into nothing. My customer was among the casualties. He was so focused on getting to the market first that he never took the time to determine what the market was, why he should be there, or what he would do when he got there. He was running with the crowd, and he ran with them right over a cliff. Like many people, my customer did not see the value in taking the time to establish his goals, priorities, and vision.

This leads us to the second reason people don't plan or set goals. Peer and social pressure set the unvoiced expectations that most people use as the baseline for their lives. People have stopped using critical-thinking skills, and they instead trust the general opinion of the public for what's important. Many people have done this without realizing it, and others have simply conformed because they care more about what's socially acceptable than what matters.

Think about it for a minute. How many beliefs do you have that are based on what society finds acceptable versus those things you have analyzed and prayed about and researched for yourself? A lot of the choices I made in my life early on were based on what my social circles viewed as normal or acceptable.

You need to make sure that the priorities and goals you set are based on your own research and beliefs. Together, we will work through some exercises that will create the process for you to do just that. I want to make sure you are not running with the crowd for the sake of running with the crowd. The crowd may be heading off the side of a cliff.

Social and peer pressure sometimes set a parameter of expectations that we use to manage our lives. If you are in school, and the students you are hanging around with tend to make Cs and Bs for grades, you will probably do the same. If your report card shows up and you have all Ds, but several of your friends have received Cs and Bs, you may sense the comparison and feel that you're out of line. On the other hand, you're also unlikely to rise to an A level. In this situation, you might determine that you've worked too hard. You can slack off a bit considering you're already outperforming your peers.

Like a thermostat, if you realize that you're above or below the expectations of your peers, your mind will kick on and bring you back into the parameters of your society.

Consider your salary as another example. If your peers are averaging $60,000–$80,000 per year, you might be asking some questions if you are only making $40,000. On the other hand, you might feel you're making too much if you are in excess of $100,000. As a result, you might feel undeserving of the salary you are making even if it is commensurate with your experience and performance. You might be less likely to work for the next raise with the assumption that you are already making too much.

I'm not making the case for finding new friends if you happen to be in a social circle with an average annual income that's below the threshold you would like. Change your expectations, not your friends. Don't base your expectations on what's acceptable within your social circle. Learn to have deep relationships with all kinds of people with different backgrounds without adopting their socially accepted expectations. If your group of friends is averaging Cs, don't use that as a baseline for your own personal goals for grades next semester. If you have the right friends, then inspire them with your new expectations.

I've witnessed this same phenomenon in sports. I grew up playing soccer, and

I've coached many teams over the years. I have known several players who had amazing talent, well beyond that of most good players. But what I found was that most of them would not work as hard as the player with average athletic ability. The average players tended to work harder and really step up in order to perform at the level of a talented player.

It was only on the rare occasion that I would see a player with amazing athletic talent who also worked as hard as he possibly could. So many people have fallen into this pattern. Perhaps this includes you. The one thing that you have a natural talent in is the one thing you don't really give your best effort to. Why? Because you don't have to. You can perform at a socially acceptable level based on your talent and limited effort. What a waste of talent and potential!

Public speaking has always come easily to me. In the past, when I would give a speech, I'd never really put forth my best effort. I never really needed to. With a little effort and limited planning, I could perform at a socially acceptable level.

Chances are you do the same thing in some area where you are gifted. Imagine for a moment what you could achieve if you were working with all your heart in the area where you are most gifted!

I encourage you to break out of your old way of thinking. It's time to become an independent thinker. You have an incredible asset at your disposal that God has blessed you with—your brain. Start comparing yourself to the level of what is possible and not to others.

The third reason people don't plan is because they think they are too busy. People mistake busyness for priority. They're running around like chickens with their heads cut off, never realizing they're running to a destination that doesn't exist because it has never been defined.

If you're too busy right now to do any planning or goal setting, then I know exactly why you are too busy. It's because you've never done any planning or goal setting! After I started my first business several years ago, I found myself getting extremely busy. The company had grown dramatically, but my partner and I had not kept up with the hiring of support personnel to accommodate the growth. As a result, we were doing the jobs of ten people.

Some other business owners gave me advice: "You need to hire some people to reduce your workload. You're going to burn yourself out at this pace."

For the longest time I didn't heed their insightful advice because I thought I was too busy to take the time to hire. Think about that logic for a minute! It doesn't take a brain surgeon to figure out that I was using bad logic, but extreme busyness can do that to you. It can distort reality and confuse you.

In order to break the cycle, you have to force yourself to step back and do some real planning, prioritization, and goal setting. Being too busy is the symptom of a lack of planning, so stop using it as your excuse. It's like saying that you are too hungry to be eating right now.

There are many other excuses that can be used as reasons to not do planning or set goals, but they are only excuses. The importance of this exercise is paramount. Please trust me on this.

CREATING A PLAN

Establishing priorities in your life will break you out of a cycle of doing things for the sake of doing things. I want to encourage you to think about what's important. What do you really care about? What do you really feel led to do, and how can you get there? Are you just going through the motions because you really don't know what else to do? I'm going to give you a plan to make a plan. Once you know the formula, you'll be able to analyze every aspect of your life, prioritize what's important, and then develop a specific plan of action for success through goal setting.

We will begin with priorities. You are going to learn a goal-setting approach in the next chapter. Before we do that, you have to first determine what's most important. It would be a shame to set and achieve a goal only to discover later that it was the wrong goal, or that it was less than it could have been.

Are you extremely busy in your life, but you do not have a sense of purpose, accomplishment, or peace? Many people are living their lives in fast-forward. They are racing from one thing to the next in an unorganized, misguided attempt to find purpose.

Let me provide an example. There are so many things that I long to do in this world. Below is just a partial list of things I'd like to accomplish:

- Memorize more key passages in the Bible
- Spend more quality time with Angie by taking several weekend trips and date nights
- Spend individual quality time with each of my children
- Take some fishing trips with my dad and brothers
- Start hunting some new game like duck, turkey, and elk
- Reconnect with several old friends I haven't seen in a long time
- Visit Germany and Virginia to do some genealogy research

- Work toward achieving my black belt in karate
- Start playing guitar again in a weekend or wedding band
- Start playing soccer on a weeknight league
- Play basketball on a church league on Tuesday nights
- Get my private pilot's license and start flying small planes
- Run in a marathon
- Write two new books on business and start-ups
- Master some new moves on a wakeboard at the lake
- Finish several home projects that I started several years ago
- Join a trap-and-skeet league
- Restore an old car in my garage with my dad
- Start a card night with several of my friends
- Join an archery club with my sons and start shooting in a league
- Start traveling around the US to see several bands in concert that I've always dreamed of seeing
- Attend several car shows a year
- Finish several projects on my hunting land
- Write some new songs and record them with some musician friends
- Teach my sons how to play guitar
- Attend several Cardinals' baseball games, Rams' football games, and Blues' hockey games each year
- Complete a master's degree in theology
- Go back for another business degree specializing in finance
- Learn Spanish
- Start a nonprofit group locally in St. Louis that helps inner-city children learn how to start new businesses

If I put the full list down, it would have taken three more pages. Can you see that it would be impossible to achieve everything that I want to do? All of the things listed are good things, but how many of them are great things? What makes the difference between the things that are good and the things that are great? My *priorities* are what make the difference.

You don't want to be in the trap of doing so many good things that you are missing the great things. This is a tough one, because it means saying no to some really cool opportunities! But you have to be able to say no to the good things in order to say yes to the great ones.

The same thing happens when you decide to get married. You may have dated a lot of good people, but you're looking for the one. The one who is great for you. You say no to a lot of good people in order to say yes to the one who is great. If you are never willing to do that, you'll never get married.

Jim Collins, author of the book *Good to Great,* makes a remarkable observation: "We don't have great schools, principally because we have good schools. We don't have great government, principally because we have good government. Few people attain great lives, in large part because it is just so easy to settle for a good life." He goes on to say, "Good is the enemy of great."[2]

Rick Warren in *The Purpose-Driven Life* says, "Stop dabbling. Stop trying to do it all. Do less. Prune away even good activities and do only that which matters most. Never confuse activity with productivity."[3]

So let's start the journey of discovering what's important to you. I'm going to first ask you to do an exercise that will require some thinking, and then you are going to answer several questions. Before you start, I recommend blocking off at least an hour. You need uninterrupted time to really do an effective job.

DETERMINING PRIORITY

You are going to need to use your imagination for this one. I want you to imagine that you only have one year to live. I know this isn't something we like to think or talk about, but it is necessary to get your mind focused on what's really important.

I want you to imagine that you have just been notified that you've got one year to live—that's twelve months, three hundred and sixty-five days. The clock starts right now. Don't worry about saying good-bye to loved ones or getting a will in place. Let's assume that's all done. Just focus on how you will live for the next three hundred and sixty-five days. Take some time and answer the following questions the best that you can.

- Who will you spend your time with? Why?
- How will you spend your time with the ones you've chosen to be with?
- Is there anything you need to work out with God?
- Are there any big decisions that need to be made?
- Is there anything you've been putting off that you need to take action on?
- Is there anyone you need to apologize to?
- What legacy are you going to leave?
- What's important now that wasn't important before? Why?

- What do you worry about?
- What were you worrying about before that you are not worrying about now?
- Is there anything you haven't done that you would like to do?
- Is there anything you've been doing that needs to stop?
- What happens to your awareness and presence in the moment? Are you more connected with what's happening or are you distant?
- Do you have any regrets? What are they?
- What are you most excited about?
- What do you want people to say about you in twelve months?
- What do you want people to know?

I hope you found this exercise enlightening. My hope is that your mind is really turning about the big things of life right now. Let me ask you this: Are you going to do anything different? Has anything changed in your life? If so, I want you to start writing it down immediately. Don't wait for tomorrow or another minute. Write down the top five things that need to change in your life right now. Do it. I'm not asking you. I'm telling you. I feel like I'm talking to my kids. Do not hesitate. Write it down.

Once you've written those things down, you are well on your way to defining your priorities. The approach that you just took should have cut right to the chase. We want to get to the top priorities and not waste any time with things that don't matter.

Now that you've put yourself in a frame of mind that is more congruent to the truly important things of your life, make a list of everything that is important to you and everything you've ever wanted to do or felt led to do. List everything that you can. This should be a fun exercise. I've provided some topic ideas below to help stimulate your brain in this direction of thinking:

- Think about your relationship to God and list anything that you would like to improve in that area.
  - Would you like to grow in your knowledge and understanding of God?
  - Is there something God has really laid on your heart to do?
- Think about your family and your relationship to them:
  - Are you married or dating someone?
  - Do you have children?

- • Consider your parents, siblings, grandparents, etc.
- • Other family members
- Close friends
- Finances
- What would you like to achieve financially?
  - • Debt free?
  - • Save for college?
  - • Investing?
- Career/work/school
  - • What goals would you like to set for your career?
  - • Would you like to make a career change?
  - • Grades or possible graduation goals?
  - • Start a new business?
- Involvement in church or nonprofit or civic service
- Health/fitness
  - • Diet/losing weight
  - • Nutrition, etc.
  - • Exercise
- Hobbies/projects
- Personal improvement
  - • Quit smoking/drinking
  - • Learn a new language
  - • Run a marathon
  - • Books to read
- Fun goals
  - • A vacation
  - • Family reunion
  - • Improvements to your house

List everything that you can. The topics above are not meant to be comprehensive, but they should give you some ideas as you are making your list. The important thing is to list everything you can think of. Don't worry about whether it is achievable or reasonable at this point. You are just trying to formulate a good list.

Once this list is complete, I want you to take at least twenty-four hours and clear your head. Then come back and think about anything you may have missed. You want to be sure you've listed everything you can possibly think of. Once you are confident in the completeness of the list, take another twenty-four hours off.

You should now have a fairly long, exhaustive list of the things you either want to do or feel you need to do. I now want you to start praying for God's wisdom and direction. You should spend some time praying about God's will for you and his goals and plans for your life. Ask God to give you a discerning heart as you start to prioritize your list. The Bible says, "Do not be foolish, but understand what the will of the Lord is."[4]

The important thing to remember as you prioritize your list is that although many things on it will not make your final list, it doesn't mean you will never attempt them. It could be that you will accomplish things on your list many years from now. But they do not need to take priority right now.

I have always dreamed of learning how to fly. It has been on my goal list for many years, but the goal of learning to fly has not taken the priority necessary to make my final list. However, I do believe that I will make flying a key goal in my life many years from now, probably after my children are on their own and out of college.

While I really have a desire to get a pilot's license, there are several things that are just more important in my life right now. As you prioritize your list, don't be afraid to say no to some good things right now. Your no today might be a yes five years from now. Who knows?

I would now like you to rank each item on your list, beginning with one for top importance and moving down through the entire list. This is where you will really start to make some decisions about what's important. You might want to go back and review your notes from the "one year to live" exercise you did. As you are working through this list, remember to ask God for wisdom.

Below are some questions that might help you in evaluating the priorities of your list:

- Does this goal match up with what's really important to me?
- Would this goal honor God and/or bring me closer to God?
- Am I willing to give up my time and energy in the pursuit of this goal?
- Can I visualize myself accomplishing this goal? Is it possible to achieve?
- How would this goal affect those people who could be involved?
- Do I have the necessary time in my schedule to accomplish this goal in my life right now?

I'll give you an example of a goal that I set several years ago and how I came to prioritize it. It's a financial goal, and I had it on my dream list for a couple of years. The goal was to become completely debt free within five years.

I really prayed about this goal for quite some time, and I truly felt that this was a desire God had laid on my heart. The goal was certainly something that honored God. It was achievable. It lined up well with what was important in my life. I was willing to sacrifice in order to make it happen, and although it was hard to visualize, I could see myself accomplishing this goal.

Once I felt I had a clear picture of the importance of the goal, I added it to my final list. I mentioned earlier that learning to fly did not make my final list. Becoming debt free was more important to me than learning to fly. If I was not willing to say no to some of the lower priority goals, then I would never have been able to accomplish the higher priority goal, which was to become debt free.

If I had not worked through this process, I would have continued to be busy with many good things, but I would have missed out on the rare, great things in my life.

Your mission now is to finalize your list of your highest priority goals. Please consider your time as a necessary component to this final list: you need to make sure that your final list conforms to the amount of time you have available. If you are working full-time and you have small children, and you determine that one of your highest priority goals is going back to school, then take your remaining goals into consideration from a time perspective. You might not have time to train for a marathon or write a book until you finish that degree. If you overcommit to a list that exceeds your time constraints, you will end up sacrificing your higher priority goals. For example, you might be training for that marathon on the weekends and never see your children.

In my own life, I created a priority list that I have used for years to assist as I prioritize my most important goals. I personally rank my priorities in this order:

- God and my relationship to him
- My relationship to Angie
- My relationship to my children
- Family
- Health
- Career/businesses/job
- Friendships
- Finances
- Personal goals

The above list is only an example. You have to make sure your priority list is congruent with what's important to you, not to me. Your priority list will become an incredible guide for you in the future, because once you've made the big decisions about what's important, you will simply defer to this list as decision points come up. For example, I will never have a career goal (number six on my list) that negatively impacts the first five items on my list. I will not sacrifice my family or my relationship to God or my health in order to achieve a career goal. I'll never sacrifice my relationship to God (number one on my list) for a goal related to my wife (number two on my list). Likewise, my wife takes precedence over my children.

I have my friendships prioritized after my career only because my career is tied very closely to my wife and children. My career is a means that I use to support my family financially. Your priority list might be different from mine, but the important thing is that it reflects what's most important to you.

Once you've established the priorities in your life, everything else will fall into its right place. Personal conflict over how you spend your time will dissipate once you know your priorities.

If you don't take the time to determine and define your priorities, then random chance will be a greater factor in how you spend your time. You will live in conflict and chaos and regret. When you are at work, you'll be wishing you were with your family. When you're with your family, you'll be questioning whether you should be doing something else. You'll find yourself physically present but mentally absent, missing out on the joy of important events because you're preoccupied with something else. Defined priorities will create presence of mind for you, because you will know you are right where you should be in that particular moment in time. You will be free to enjoy and savor every moment of life.

CREATING A MISSION STATEMENT

Once you've identified and ranked your priorities, you can use a personal mission statement to document and define your game plan for your life. Great entrepreneurs and business owners use corporate mission statements all the time in order to position their organizations for great success, but unfortunately, most individuals do not take the same approach in their personal lives. I assure you there is no corporation of greater worth than your own life! If the most successful corporations are using mission statements, then you should consider doing the same.

Here are a few examples of great organizations that have used effective mission statements:

- Nike, Inc. currently uses this as their mission: "To bring inspiration and innovation to every athlete in the world."[5]
- Starbucks defines this as their mission: "To inspire and nurture the human spirit—one person, one cup and one neighborhood at a time."[6]
- The United States, in the Preamble to the Constitution, defines a mission for the country in this way: "We the people of the United States, in order to form a more perfect Union, establish justice, insure domestic tranquility, provide for the common defense, promote the general welfare, and secure the blessings of liberty to ourselves and our posterity, do ordain and establish this Constitution for the United States of America."[7]

Successful organizations recognize the incredible power that exists in mission statements, and successful individuals have discovered that same value. Benjamin Franklin established a personal mission statement by listing out the values he wanted to exhibit in his life.[8] Gandhi used a personal mission statement to define what he would do and not do in several areas of his life.[9] Michael Jordan has utilized a personal mission statement to become one of the greatest basketball players in the history of the game.[10]

Personal mission statements provide focus, motivation, clarity, practical application, and direction as you work to live out your most important priorities. They should clearly define what is most important to you and how you will live your life, and they should be short, clear, and concise.

As you write your personal mission statement, take some time to answer the following questions. Your answers to these questions will provide the foundation for your mission statement.

- What are my two or three greatest strengths/talents/abilities?
- What am I passionate about?
- Who matters most in my life?
- If I knew I could not fail, and I could do anything that I wanted with unlimited resources and time, what would I do?
- What impact do I want to make on the people who matter most in my life?
- Is there anything I believe God is calling me to do?

Take some time to write a rough draft of your personal mission statement. Once you have a rough draft, ask a few people you respect, trust, and know well to review it. They may have some great insight for you, and they can be extremely helpful in shaping your mission statement into a concise and clear document.

Several years ago, we wrote a family mission statement, and I have included it as an example for you. We spent several weeks thinking and praying about what was most important to our family before finally defining this as our family mission statement:

We will be a family committed first and foremost to Jesus Christ, recognizing that he created us and chose to save us. We will love Christ with all our hearts, minds, and souls, and we will seek to serve him in all we do. We will also seek to love each other unconditionally. We will always put each other above our own needs and desires. We will always encourage one another and cheer each other on. We will defend and protect each other and serve with gratitude and love. We will be passionate and excited to live each day to its fullest, always having fun and enjoying life. We will be disciplined and hardworking, never taking for granted the potential and abilities God has given us. A godly wisdom and fear of the Lord will be our guide and lighthouse. We will take the lead when called to lead. We will not be afraid, always willing to stand for what's right, even when we must stand alone. We will seek adventure, taking calculated risks to live out our dreams and God-given desires. We will live with integrity and honesty, and we will strive to model a sense of character and trust. We will never give up nor ever feel insignificant, but instead we will recall our heritage—a heritage of ancestors who came to America for religious freedom. We will remain steadfast and persistent, always knowing that we can achieve whatever it is we have chosen to accomplish. Defeat will never turn us back from the road we have been called on, but we will always look for ways to learn and grow. In all things, we will always be full of love. We will also seek rest and refuge in God's protection and in the quiet moments. Daily meditation on God's Word and prayer with him will keep us focused, humble, and of a renewed mind and spirit. We will be only what God has made us to be.

Once we completed our family mission statement, we summarized it so that we could quickly remember the primary points: "Honor God, Work Hard, Laugh

Often." We then had our mission statement summary painted over the door in our kitchen so we could see it every day. Whenever one of my children happens to fall out of step with our mission statement, I will point to the kitchen wall and remind them. It is a powerful reminder of who we are and what we stand for. Likewise, I encourage you to summarize your mission statement and then put it somewhere visible. The daily reminder will have a powerful impact on your life as you live out your most important priorities.

CHAPTER 6

Goals

"Give me a stock clerk with a goal and I'll give you a man who will make history. Give me a man with no goals and I'll give you a stock clerk."

J.C. PENNEY

The great entrepreneurs have always been effective at setting and accomplishing great goals. Fred Smith, FedEx founder and CEO, came up with an idea for overnight express delivery while in college in the early 1960s. Smith wrote a paper about the idea for a project in one of his classes. It has been reported that his professor was not impressed, and Smith received a lackluster grade for the paper.[1] Despite this setback, Fred Smith did not give up on the idea of starting a company that would provide overnight express delivery.

Today, FedEx is a thirty-billion-dollar company with operations around the world. Smith provides some insight on how he accomplished such amazing things: "If your business revolves around one idea, keep that idea foremost. Hammer away at it." Fred Smith knew exactly what he wanted to do, and he was extremely effective at keeping that one thing his primary focus.

The entire process of setting goals takes an idea and shines a spotlight in your mind on that particular idea every day. When an idea takes center stage in your mind, you now have focus. Goal setting creates focus. Focus is a very powerful thing, because a person's actions almost always come from that person's focus. This is the real secret of goal setting, and it's the reason great entrepreneurs have used this process with such great results.

God, the Creator of all things, reveals this great secret in the Bible: "Do not conform to the pattern of this world, but be transformed by the renewing of your mind. Then you will be able to test and approve what God's will is—his good, pleasing and perfect will."[2] If you want to change your actions, you have to start by changing your mind, by renewing your mind. Goal setting begins first in the mind and then leads to action. If you can control the focus of your mind, you can control your actions.

Fred Smith kept his idea for FedEx at the forefront of his mind, and this process was a key ingredient to his success. John Mayer, a Grammy Award–winning musician, became so focused on guitar as a child that his parents took him to see a psychiatrist twice just to make sure he was all right. Mayer's singular focus on music and guitar has paid him some serious dividends![3]

In 1504, Michelangelo completed the statue of David, one of the most renowned works of art from the Renaissance. When asked how he sculpted such an amazing piece, it is reported that Michelangelo replied, "I eliminated everything that was not David."

When your mind becomes focused on the important things in your life, you will not only begin to accomplish amazing things, but you will be accomplishing those things that are most important.

You are now going to learn a powerful goal-setting approach that will impact you in an incredible way. This process is the culmination of the findings of many great achievers, entrepreneurs, and leaders in addition to my own enhancements, and I believe it is the most cutting-edge, effective goal-setting strategy available. Many of the greatest accomplishments in history were made possible as a result of the principles outlined in the following seven steps.

The Formula for Setting Goals

Step 1: Paint the Picture. In the first step, you need to specifically define what the goal is. It is imperative that you be specific. Generic goals are ineffective. A goal to "be rich" is essentially useless, because it is too vague. Instead, you could have the following goal: "I will become debt free by paying off my house, car, credit-card balance, and student loans."

The specifics outline exactly what you are planning to accomplish. If your goal is simply to be rich, then you really haven't defined what it is that you intend to do. What does "rich" even mean? Make sure you are being very specific.

Once you define the specifics of your goal, it is important to paint the picture. You need to visualize exactly what accomplishing this goal would mean. It's important to see it in your mind as if it has already been achieved. Meditate for a moment on the completion of the goal. What does it feel like? Can you see it? Imagine the rush of accomplishing this goal.

Painting the picture is a powerful process that advertisers use consistently to sell products. Car dealers, for example, plan big-tent events with BBQ and balloons in order to entice potential customers to their lot. Once people are on the lot, they start to do something they probably did not intend to do when they smelled the BBQ and pulled into the parking lot—they start to look at the beautiful new cars for sale.

I love cars, and Angie has banned me from all car lots for this very reason. The second I see one of those brand-new Dodge Challengers in black with black leather interior and chrome wheels, I start to picture myself driving that car. I can smell the leather and imagine the thrust of engaging the accelerator. I start to visualize what it would be like to have that car in my garage.

Advertisers use this approach when selling vacations. What do they do? They show you amazing pictures of the beach and the dark blue water with families running hand in hand through the sand and surf.

Advertisers help paint the picture when selling exercise equipment. They don't just show you the particular machine they are hoping to sell, but they show you a person with the body you hope to have.

Can you sense the difference between simply talking about something and visualizing it? Painting the picture stimulates the brain in an extremely powerful way. You can harness this same power when you take the time to visualize the specifics of your goal and paint the picture on the canvas of your mind. You will initiate the first step of incredible accomplishment when you paint the picture, because you will know exactly what you are shooting for.

Step 2: Ask the Why Question. This step involves asking why this goal is important to you. This is one of the most important steps in the entire process, because once you know why you are doing something, you will do whatever it takes to figure out how to accomplish it. Answering the why question is essential to defining the importance of a particular goal.

If I have a goal of eating healthy and exercising on a regular basis, then I have to know why this goal is important. Am I setting this goal because I somehow think it's what I'm supposed to do? I might say to myself, "I guess I should be healthy. Everyone lists that as important, so I guess it should be important to me as well." That answer is not an effective why answer.

Instead, you need to really define why this goal is so important to you. I'll give you an example. Health is an important goal for me. Unfortunately, my family struggles with high cholesterol and high blood pressure. I've had several family members suffer from heart attacks in middle age. My health is directly tied to my family. I want to be healthy because I want to live to see my children grow up and have children of their own. I not only want to be alive, but I want to enjoy it. I don't want to be confined to a hospital bed or medical equipment. I also want to have more energy in my life. I have a lot of worthy goals that I'm excited about pursuing, but I can't do that if I have limited energy and I'm out of shape.

Do you see how I've answered the why question? I've given very specific reasons that are important to me. Answering the why question is one of the greatest secrets to accomplishing great goals. In fact, you may have practiced this principle in your own life without even realizing it.

Many years ago, my uncle was in terrible shape. He ate terrible foods, never exercised, smoked, drank alcohol, and rarely saw the doctor. In his midforties, he had a massive heart attack.

Once he recovered and was out of the hospital, my uncle was a changed man. He changed his entire diet. He started exercising every day. He quit smoking and drinking, and he never missed regular checkups with his doctor. He lost an enormous amount of weight. He looked great, and you would have never guessed he had been so out of shape a few years before.

So what happened to my uncle? I'll break it down for you: he answered the why question. His goal was to get healthy, but the key to his success was that he knew why. Once you know why, you'll do everything you can to figure out how. Do you see the power of this principle?

I consistently use this step with my children to get them thinking about why they should achieve a particular goal. I recently asked my youngest son, Peyton, why he wanted to learn karate. He answered, "So I can protect my girlfriend." I laughed when he answered with that, but at least he is thinking about why. Answer the why question, and you've got 80 percent of the goal-setting process accomplished.

Step 3: Create a Specific Plan to Achieve the Goal. I mentioned earlier that the experts report that only 3 percent of the population do any kind of goal setting. Even fewer take the time to create a plan for how to achieve their goals. You have to be able to map the trip from where you are now to where you want to be when the goal is accomplished.

The goal is your destination, and your plan is the road map for how to get there. Your plans will change, but the goal should remain constant. It's all right to modify and adjust your plans, but you will live in chaos if your goals continue to change.

I have a friend who's a pilot in the US Air Force, Lieutenant Colonel Mickey Tate. Mickey says that when you determine your destination, you then create a flight plan. When the plane gets into the air and heads toward the destination, the pilot is constantly making adjustments every few minutes to keep the plane en route. It is very common for the pilot to make minor adjustments and modifications to keep the plane on course—air traffic control may alter the route for various reasons, or weather along the path may cause a change in course—but only in extreme and dire cases does a pilot change the plane's destination. Your goal-setting practices should be very similar. Once you set the goals, they should be locked down. In some rare cases, you may decide to change a goal, but this should not be a common practice.

Your plans for accomplishing a goal must be specific. I set a goal several years ago to do a Bible study every day. Here's what my plan looked like:

- I will get up thirty minutes early every morning at 6:15 a.m. and work through the following studies:
    - *Experiencing God* by Henry Blackaby
    - *A Heart Like His* by Beth Moore
- I will keep a prayer list and spend ten minutes in prayer every morning and twenty minutes working through a study.
- If I miss a morning, I will plan to do the Bible study during my lunch break or later in the evening as a backup.
- I will also work to memorize Scripture. I will plan to work on this in the car, utilizing the Bible on CD. I will maximize my downtime while driving to meetings to memorize passages of Scripture.
    - I'll finish memorizing chapter 5 of the book of James
    - Memorize Psalm 139
- I will have Angie ask me every evening if I've completed my Bible study for the day in order to keep me accountable.

This game plan worked fairly well for me, but I did make modifications. Getting up thirty minutes early did not work out as I had planned, so I made a contingency plan for doing the Bible study at lunch or in the evening.

Notice the specifics of my plan. I didn't just make the goal to have a Bible study, but I spelled out a very specific plan that included what I was going to do, when I was going to do it, and how I would do it. These components are critical to accomplishing the goal.

Step 4: Anticipate the Obstacles. With every goal you set, there will be obstacles. It's important to identify the obstacles and be aware of how you will overcome them.

This planning will put you in a proactive posture, and you will not be demoralized when the obstacles come your way. They will come. I promise you. You don't accomplish great things without obstacles. So plan and prepare for them.

Mary Kay Ash, founder of Mary Kay Cosmetics, once said, "When you reach an obstacle, turn it into an opportunity. You have the choice. You can overcome and be a winner, or you can allow it to overcome you and be a loser. The choice is yours and yours alone." If you are going to make the choice to overcome the obstacles that are certain to come your way, then make those choices in advance.

One of the reasons the United States Special Operations Forces are so effective is that they spend a lot of time in their preparation for missions determining all possible obstacles and potential setbacks and then formulating contingency plans. When a Special Operations Force commences a mission, they usually have a very specific game plan. However, they also always have several contingency plans for any obstacles they may encounter. The benefit is that when obstacles arise in the middle of a mission, they can quickly adapt and make the necessary adjustments. There is a saying among these teams: "The more you sweat during planning, the less you bleed during execution."[4] The absolute worst time to consider contingencies is when you are in the middle of executing a plan. It is much better if you have considered the possible obstacles in advance and prepared accordingly.

This is a step often overlooked on one side and overanalyzed on the other. If you are a glass-half-full person, your inclination will be to overlook this critical step. Positive people struggle to consider everything that could go wrong. Such thinking runs counter to the core of their personality. If this is your predisposition, then force yourself to carry out this exercise. If you do not, you might be shocked and paralyzed when you reach your first obstacle. You may find yourself in a defensive posture looking for a quick way out. The result will not be good.

If you are a glass-half-empty person, then you will have no problem at all considering everything that could possibly go wrong. The danger of this exercise is that you may use all the possible obstacles as reasons to abandon your goal before you ever begin! The value of listing all the possible obstacles will materialize when you are able to strike a balance between the two extremes.

As you list potential obstacles, think about your contingency plans and how you will make adjustments. You will not only be equipped to make the necessary modifications, but you will also dramatically increase your level of confidence and your ability to achieve the goal. Preparation breeds confidence.

Once you have taken action and considered all the possible obstacles and created contingency plans to accommodate those potential obstacles, realize that there will be unforeseen obstacles that will rear their ugly heads at the worst times, and you will be faced with a decision. Your action in those moments will be the difference between success and failure.

These situations will reveal your level of resolve and tenacity, but with some creative thinking, you can maneuver through the obstacles. Persistence is often considered a great attribute of great entrepreneurs; however, Steven K. Scott provides a critical insight into this idea in his book *Mentored by a Millionaire*:

> Most people have a dangerous misconception of what tenacity or persistence is. They associate it with the adage, "If at first you don't succeed, try, try again." This concept of persistence is like hitting a brick wall, falling down, then getting back up and hitting it over and over again. That is not persistence, it's stupidity.[5]

Persistence is an amazing quality when it is fused with innovative adjustments. Thomas Edison is a great example of overcoming obstacles through the use of persistence with innovative adjustments and creative thinking.

Edison once said, "Negative results are just what I want. They're just as valuable to me as positive results. I can never find the thing that does the job best until I find the ones that don't." He also stated, "I have not failed. I've just found ten thousand ways that won't work." Edison's persistence was never about taking the same approach over and over again.[6] Albert Einstein's definition of insanity was doing the same thing over and over again and expecting different results. The average person believes persistence is taking the same approach over and over, and they quickly give up when they realize the same approach is netting them the same results.

As you face obstacles in the pursuit of your goal, you will need to use creative thinking in order to make innovative adjustments. Persistence will be the key ingredient to not abandoning new approaches and modifications. Edison, who used the creative process to evolve and create better potential solutions until finally achieving the approach that proved successful, once said, "Many of life's failures are people who did not realize how close they were to success when they gave up."

When I started my first company in technology, my business partner and I modified the business plan and overall approach of the company numerous times before finally settling on a profitable strategy. We made many adjustments along the way as we monitored what was working and what was not working.

Step 5: Create Urgency. Urgency is a potent force, because it is usually produced by some degree of leverage. Leverage leads to urgency and urgency leads to action, usually immediate action. Think about this for a moment. Imagine the windshield wipers on your car have quit working. The weather forecast is predicting sunshine with no chance of rain for the next week. You know you need to get the wipers fixed, but how urgent is it that you get them fixed soon? Now imagine that your windshield wipers have quit working and a thunderstorm is imminent in the next few hours. Has the urgency changed? Of course it has, because the looming storm has created leverage. If you don't get your wipers fixed in the next few hours, you will either be without a vehicle or in danger for the duration of the storm.

Here's another example: A few years ago I was working in an office building, and the fire alarms went off. I knew that I would have to exit the building, but I assumed it was only a test, so I was not in any hurry to leave. I checked a few more e-mails and casually left my office. As I entered the hallway toward the elevator, people were yelling from the other end of the hallway that the building was on fire. Can you guess how my urgency changed upon learning that news? I went from a slow, leisurely stroll to a full run for the stairs. The leverage of possibly dying in a fire created the urgency for me to take immediate action and get out of there fast.

If you can create urgency around your most important goals, then you will find yourself taking instantaneous action. The reason most people fail to accomplish their goals is that they never feel the necessary urgency to do so.

One very effective way to create urgency is through the practice of setting dates. Think about a time when you were in school and you had a term paper due or a big test coming. If you were like me, you probably found yourself working harder the closer you came to the deadline. A deadline or date for achievement creates that pressure, and it gives you a clear picture of when you expect to accomplish your goal.

Date setting can be used in project-oriented goals and in ongoing goals. For example, becoming healthy is an ongoing goal, so you may be wondering how you would set a date on it. Use deadlines to create urgency around components of your goal. As an example, exercise may be a component of your goal to get healthy. You might want to set a goal of running two miles within six months. You might only be able to run one mile today, but your goal is to get to two. Set a date for when you will hit that second mile, and then set a date for when you will hit the third. Set a date for where you would like your resting heartbeat, cholesterol level, and blood pressure to be. Deadlines can be used in several areas to create the drive for accomplishing the goal.

Another way to create urgency is to consider the consequences of not accomplishing your goal. One of my top goals is to have an outstanding relationship with each of my children. I have created several plans for how to be involved in their lives, but these plans do not have an inherent urgency to them. Usually our most important goals are not urgent in nature, especially when we do not consider future consequences. One way that I create urgency around my goals with my children is to imagine how they will turn out as adults if I fail as their father. This process has produced incredible results for creating urgency in my life!

Urgency is the spark that ignites the fuel of your goals. Use it to spur the necessary action you must take in the process of making your goals reality.

Step 6: Document Your Goals and Review Them Daily. Once you've worked through the first five steps, you need to document each of your major goals and then review them every day. I use Outlook Calendar on my computer as a means for reviewing my goals. I set up a recurring appointment on my calendar for every morning at 7 a.m. I marked it private so that only I can see it, and then I typed all my goals into the appointment. Every morning I get into the office, and I review my goals.

Another option is to print or write out your goals and place a copy in the glove box of your car or in your planner or some place that will be visible to you on a daily basis. Whenever you arrive at work or school or wherever you are headed, pull them out and review them. It takes me about three minutes every day to review my major goals. This is very important because it keeps your top objectives at the front of your mind on a daily basis.

I've been using this format of goal setting now for almost fifteen years. In preparation for this chapter, I went back and reviewed my goals from years ago. I was amazed to see that I've achieved or exceeded virtually every goal I have set for myself. Goal setting is a powerful process that will change your entire life.

Once you have listed everything that's important to you and then prioritized the list and then worked through the six steps of goal setting on each major goal, there's one thing left to do:

Step 7: Just Do It. Several years ago, Nike ran a great commercial with the slogan, "Just Do It." I can't stress the importance of taking action enough. Discipline is the key. There's no better way to describe what you must do next, so I'll let Nike's slogan do the work: just do it. Go out and take action on the goals you've set.

There will be days when you don't feel like it, and there will be many days when it won't be convenient. Those are the days when you have to decide: you are either going to live with purpose and meaning, or you're going to be a slave to your feelings and live in mediocrity.

Jim Rohn once said, "We must all suffer from one of two pains: the pain of discipline or the pain of regret. The difference is discipline weighs ounces while regret weighs tons."

Nolan Bushnell, the founder of Atari and Chuck E. Cheese's, described the power of action: "A lot of people have ideas, but there are few who decide to do something about them now. Not tomorrow. Not next week. But today. The true entrepreneur is a doer, not a dreamer." You do not have to be an entrepreneur to be a doer and a person of action. This principle rings true regardless of your profession. So just do it.

Once you've worked through the powerful seven steps outlined above, you will reap numerous benefits. Goal setting will provide a focus on what's really important in your life, and it will allow you to perform at a higher level.

Zig Ziglar refers to one advantage of goal setting as the ability to free your right brain. In Zig's book *Over the Top,* he writes:

The best analogy I can give you is the superbly conditioned and gifted athlete who is so disciplined and committed to the fundamentals of the game that he or she is free to be at the creative best. When unique situations arise where the athlete must improvise to make the big play, coaches of gifted athletes will typically say, "You can't coach that." Michael Jordan, for example, was confronted a number of times in every game he played with a new situation. It might have been the number of opponents around him, the number of players supporting him close by, the exact distance of the ball from the hoop, or a number of other little things that would make the situations uniquely—even if minutely—different from previously encountered situations. Because Michael was so drilled in the fundamentals of dribbling, passing, shooting, faking, pumping, and looking off, he, with his superb athletic skills, could be creative in the way he handled the truly unique situations that arose.[7]

When you have the big questions answered in your life and you are living in discipline, you allow your mind the creative freedom it needs to do great things. You are putting yourself in the position to win and win big.

SHOOT FOR THE MOON

One of the questions I always get from people regarding goal setting is this: "Should I set really big goals or should I set small, achievable goals?" It is a valid question, and I know many people have struggled with this thought process.

Many people have reasoned that setting a big goal will probably lead to disappointment in the end, and therefore you should set more realistic, achievable goals. You will find that goal-setting experts rarely recommend setting really big goals. Steven K. Scott writes about this idea:

> One of the greatest falsehoods ever propagated by motivational speakers, writers, and educators is the crippling concept found at the heart of their teachings on the subject of goal setting. In a nutshell, these well-intentioned experts tell us that we should only set reasonable and timely achievable goals. They are afraid that if we set goals that are too lofty, we won't achieve them, which may cause us to give up on those goals and ultimately abandon the goal-setting process altogether... If your only hope is to experience a moderate to good improvement in an area of your life or in a particular endeavor, then setting reasonable and achievable goals will help you do just that.[8]

I want you to quit playing it safe and really go for it. Setting small, safe goals will net you small, safe results. You are capable of doing amazing things, and your goals should reflect that potential. It is important that you stretch out and plan and prepare for the big goals. The seven steps you just learned will equip you with the strategy for accomplishing big goals with an achievable and deliberate approach. The actual steps of your pursuit of a goal should always be achievable and realistic. However, the overall goal should be big and ambitious. The approach of the seven steps toward the big goal is the realistic means by which you can make steady progress.

Theodore Roosevelt once said, "Far better it is to dare mighty things, to win glorious triumphs, even though checkered by failure than to rank with those poor spirits who neither enjoy much nor suffer much, because they live in a grey twilight that knows not victory nor defeat." Friedrich Von Schiller said, "He that is overcautious will accomplish little." Napoleon Hill said, "Whatever the mind can conceive and believe it can achieve."

I challenge you today to consider the impossible. It is often what we consider to be impossible that God makes possible. The Bible says, "In all your ways acknowledge Him, and He shall direct your paths."[9] God's plans are always great, and our plans never compare. When our plans are God's plans, we are positioned for greatness. The Bible says, "There is no wisdom, no insight, no plan that can succeed against the Lord."[10]

You are free today to reset your expectations and broaden the idea of what is possible. God loves to demonstrate his greatness when we submit our lives to him. If you choose to seek his plans over your own, then start thinking big—really big. Every great entrepreneur who ever achieved amazing things set amazing goals.

As you work through the goal-setting process, I want you to consider not what is probable, but rather what is possible. As you work through the seven steps of goal setting, ask yourself this question: "If I could accomplish this goal, what would be my dream scenario?"

If you have a goal to improve your marriage, don't set the bar at mediocrity. This would be an example of a safe, realistic, mediocre goal: "I want to have better communication with my spouse and try not to argue as much as we do now." You would not exactly be reaching for the stars with a goal like that! Instead, think big. "I intend to have the best marriage possible in which my spouse and I are best friends and madly in love with each other. We will place each other's needs above our own and be a model for an amazing, healthy marriage to others."

If you are in a struggling marriage right now, a goal like this may seem like an impossible feat. I guarantee you it will be an impossible feat if you are not able to dream big and use the goal-setting process to move from where you are now to where you want to be in the future. But it is not impossible if you do.

Big Goals Are Achieved with Incremental Daily Actions

As you create your goals and dream big, you may find yourself feeling overwhelmed as you begin to take action. As you work through the seven steps, remember to take incremental steps every day. If I need to save $100,000, it will be impossible to do in a week's time; but if I save a little each day and invest the interest, I can save $100,000 easily over a specified period of time. Saint Augustine once said, "You aspire to great things? Begin with little ones."

Several years ago, I started an exercise routine with a friend who was a fitness trainer. As we started a weight-training regimen, I was ready to take on the world. He wisely instructed me to begin with lower weights and a handful of movements. I could easily have taken on more, but he wanted to me to start slow and build incrementally. Many people burn themselves out at the gym on the first day, and they have a tough time returning the next day when they are sore and exhausted.

Your approach to goal setting should be very similar. Your goals should be substantial, but your actions every day should build incrementally. If you have a goal to run ten miles, you don't go out and try to run the ten miles on your first day. Remember that small, incremental steps every single day are the key to incredible accomplishment.

When I started my job at Johnson & Johnson, I had a lot of work to do. My territory was the worst-performing geography in the district, and I was anxious to turn the tide in the first week. My boss shared this adage with me, and it has proven true: "By the inch it is a cinch, but by the yard, it is hard." As you take daily action on your goals, you will be building endurance, confidence and routine. A routine is essential to creating discipline. As I mentioned earlier, one of my goals is to study the Bible and spend time in prayer every day. I spend about thirty minutes every day reading God's Word and praying. Over the course of a month, I have spent about fifteen hours in Bible study. That process has become part of my routine, and it is a way of life, not just an event. The effectiveness would be minimal if I tried to do a fifteen-hour Bible study once a month. George Washington once said, "Discipline is the soul of an army. It makes small numbers formidable; procures success to the weak, and esteem to all."

Decide today to take action on your most important goals, and begin by putting the seven-step process to work. Yogi Berra once said, "If you don't know where you are going, you might not get there." Make the commitment today to decide where you are going and take that first step on an amazing journey of accomplishment.

CHAPTER 7

Ability to See Opportunity Others Do Not See

"If opportunity doesn't knock, build a door."

MILTON BERLE

O f all the amazing attributes of the great entrepreneurs, the ability to see opportunity others do not see is the one that intrigues me the most. Have you ever wondered how the great entrepreneurs are able to see opportunity the entire world has overlooked? Perhaps you've asked yourself, "Why didn't I see that?" or "Why didn't I think of that?"

Henry Ford exhibited this quality almost a century ago when he recognized an opportunity that the entire automotive industry had missed. At that time there were hundreds of automotive manufacturers who were all building cars for one segment of the population: the rich. Ford had an idea to mass-produce lower-cost automobiles in order to accommodate the masses. Ford Motor Company introduced the Model T in 1908, and by 1928 one out of every two cars in the world was a Ford.[1]

Howard Schultz, the CEO of Starbucks, is another example of an entrepreneur who saw opportunity others missed. Schultz was working for Starbucks in the early 1980s as the director of marketing when he recognized the prevalence of coffee bars in Italy after traveling there on a business trip. At this time Starbucks was not the type of coffee business we all know and love. Starbucks provided coffee to fine restaurants and other outlets, but it did not provide the espresso/milk-based drinks in a coffeehouse atmosphere as it does today. While in Italy, Schultz was amazed at the popularity of espresso drinks and the idea of coffee bars serving as a place for people to meet and hang out.

He tried to convince the owners of Starbucks to offer espresso drinks as an additional offering, but the owners were not interested. They did not see the same opportunity he did, and Schultz left to start his own company. A few years later, the Starbucks management team decided to sell the Starbucks retail unit to Schultz. Over the next couple of decades, Schultz would grow Starbucks into one of the greatest and most popular brands in the world, creating a movement of coffeehouses across the United States. I must admit I have contributed to the Starbucks success as a frequent customer and admirer of their coffee.[2]

Howard Schultz recognized an opportunity that others completely missed. As a result, millions of customers enjoy their Starbucks coffee every day, and Schultz is considered to be one of the richest people in the United States according to *Forbes* magazine.

You probably have never heard of Ray Kroc, but I'll bet you've heard of McDonald's. Ray Kroc met Richard and Maurice McDonald in the mid-1950s. At that time, the McDonald brothers had eight restaurants. Kroc saw an amazing opportunity. The baby-boomer generation and the interstate system were changing the culture. Families were on the go, from baseball games to soccer practice to ballet. Kroc recognized an opportunity for fast-food restaurants and the potential to grow through franchising, but the McDonald brothers did not see this same opportunity. Richard and Maurice ended up selling McDonald's to Kroc for less than three million dollars.[3] Under Kroc's leadership, McDonald's grew into the world's largest chain of hamburger fast-food restaurants, and today it serves sixty-four million customers in one hundred and nineteen countries each day, with approximately twenty-six billion dollars in revenue annually.[4]

I could provide one example after another of great entrepreneurs who were able to see opportunity others could not see. The value of this one ability is priceless. Imagine for a moment that you could possess and apply this same entrepreneurial attribute in your personal life. What could you do with this skill? Imagine the impact you could make in your children if you started to see potential in them that others couldn't see. Consider the influence this attribute would have in your marriage if you could see potential in your spouse that no one else could distinguish. Picture the impact you could have in your career or job if you started to see opportunities that others in your company or industry were missing. Imagine the impact you could make in the ministry you serve if you started to recognize opportunities and needs that others were missing.

Regardless of your talents and present abilities, you can learn and apply this entrepreneurial attribute in your life. It's not a supernatural talent that only the great entrepreneurs possess—I assure you! Anyone can learn and apply this way of seeing.

Every day, great opportunities are missed because they were not visible to the average person despite the abundance of clues. These opportunities are begging to be discovered. They are calling your name every day. At times they are but a whisper, and at other times they are yelling from the rooftops. The average person misses the signs of opportunity, not because of a lack of intelligence, education, or position, but because he doesn't know what to look for.

The following quotes, while somewhat obvious in hindsight, are entertaining examples of missed opportunity:

- "We don't like their sound, and guitar music is on the way out."—Dick Rowe, executive with Decca Recording Company, commenting on The Beatles in 1962 just before they were signed.
- "I do not believe the introduction of motor-cars will ever affect the riding of horses."—Mr. Scott Montague
- "Airplanes are interesting toys but of no military value."—Marshall Ferdinand Foch
- "Stocks have reached what looks like a permanently high plateau."—Irving Fisher, professor of economics at Yale University, commenting on the stock market on October 21, 1929, just days before the stock market crash and the beginning of the Great Depression.
- "This 'telephone' has too many shortcomings to be seriously considered as a means of communication. The device is inherently of no value to us."—Western Union internal memo, 1876.
- *Gone with the Wind* is going to be the biggest flop in Hollywood history. I'm glad it'll be Clark Gable who's falling flat on his nose, not me."—Gary Cooper.

Mark Twain once wrote, "I was seldom able to see an opportunity until it had ceased to be one." In this chapter, you are going to learn how to discern an opportunity before it ceases to be one.

In 1981, Steven Spielberg started work on a new movie that would be a huge box-office hit: *E.T.: The Extra-Terrestrial*. In the movie, the main character, Elliott, befriends an extraterrestrial who is stranded on Earth and hides him in his bedroom. The film's original script included a scene in which Elliott would use M&Ms to lure the extraterrestrial out of the woods.

Spielberg sent representatives to meet with Mars, Inc., the makers of M&Ms, in order to work out a deal to use the candy in the movie. The Mars, Inc. executives chose to pass on the opportunity, and so Spielberg's representatives approached Hershey, the makers of Reese's Pieces, instead. Jack Dowd, Hershey's vice president, recognized the opportunity before him. (Spielberg was not an unknown at this time; he had already written and directed movies like *Jaws* and *Raiders of the Lost Ark*.)

Dowd worked out a deal with Spielberg, and the movie was shot with Reese's Pieces instead of M&Ms. Just before *E.T.* was released in the summer of 1982, Reese's Pieces sales were down. Within two weeks of the movie's release, sales of the candy tripled. *E.T.* catapulted Reese's Pieces sales, and Hershey was hailed as brilliant for seizing the opportunity. On the other hand, Mars, Inc. was embarrassed by the missed opportunity, so much so that it later implied it had never received an offer for *E.T.*[5]

By nature, missed opportunity is in many ways hard to quantify—but I am confident the losses are significant. We will never know what incredible things were in store for us had we seized the opportunity. In the majority of cases, opportunities have passed by without us ever knowing. As tragic as this may be, I want you to know that opportunities are like buses—there will always be another on its way! When you master the invaluable skills of discerning and capitalizing on opportunities, the only opportunities you will ever miss will be the ones you choose to pass on. The elusive, indiscernible, undetectable opportunity will never again evade you.

ASKING EFFECTIVE QUESTIONS

The first component to identifying opportunity is the use of questions. Questions are extremely powerful because they activate the cognitive abilities of your brain. Think about it for a moment. When you are thinking, you are usually asking yourself questions. Your brain uses questions to assess and determine what is happening at any given moment in time. For example, let's assume you are driving in a car and suddenly your car is struck and starts to spin out of control. What goes through your head in that situation? You ask questions: What just happened? Am I all right? What do I do next? Who else is involved? Or you attend a party and you've just arrived. You might ask the following questions: Who do I know? Who should I talk to? What should we talk about? Am I accepted here? Is this enjoyable, or should I leave?

Thinking is largely made up of questions; they are how the brain evaluates and assesses reality. God wired us this way, and that is why Jesus often used questions in his communication with those around him. When Jesus sat with his disciples, he asked them, "Who do the crowds say I am?" and then he asked them, "Who do you say I am?" Peter answered the latter question with, "God's Messiah."[6] Jesus could have just told the disciples "I am the Messiah," but instead he used a question to stimulate the brains of the disciples to think and reason.

The power of the question is an amazing thing, but there is a difference between effective questions and disempowering questions. The purpose of a good question is to stimulate the brain to reason and think and solve problems. A disempowering question is one that implies a negative answer in the very nature of the question itself. For example, I may ask myself, "Why do I always fail?" By nature, this particular question implies that I do always fail. I'm just asking my brain to provide reasons why that is true. This is an example of a very destructive question.

Another example of a disempowering question is this: "Why do people hate me?" Again, this question implies that people hate me, and what I am really asking for is reasons to support that assumption. I have not challenged my brain to provide any constructive solutions, but rather to provide evidence for what I already believe to be true. Many, many people are in the habit of thinking this way without being aware of its destructive nature.

The use of effective questions, on the other hand, has the potential to change everything because it changes the way you use your most potent tool, your brain. Once you pose a question, your brain will go to work in search of an answer. It is absolutely amazing what the mind is capable of. It is important to note that the brain doesn't always generate a solution immediately. I have often asked myself a question only to arrive at a solution a few hours and sometimes days later, so you may need to be patient. I am often amazed at what my feeble brain can deliver when I've asked the right questions!

Now that you realize there is more than one way to ask yourself questions, I want to equip you to ask effective, empowering questions. An empowering question includes an open query that does not imply an answer inherently, and it should direct the mind in a positive way. I'll provide a few examples:

- How can I become healthy and fit and have fun at the same time?
- How can I grow in my relationship with God in an exciting and adventurous way?

- What can I do to be the best father I can possibly be while maintaining a balance of discipline and love?
- How can I have an amazing marriage and demonstrate to my wife that I love her on a consistent basis?
- What can we do to make this happen in a way that meets my needs and yours in this particular situation?

Do you recognize the power of these questions? They are not closed, but open. They are open for a potential solution, and they do not impose or imply a negative assumption. I have personally used these questions in my own life, and I have been astonished at the answers my mind has created. When you begin to ask yourself empowering questions instead of disempowering questions in the important areas of your life, your brain will go to work and create amazing solutions.

The power of questions is the first component to seeing opportunity, because instead of assuming what is not possible, you are now asking what is possible. Once you train yourself to think differently through the use of effective questions, you can move to the second component of seeing opportunity. But before you do, take ten to fifteen minutes to create five empowering questions that you can begin asking yourself every day that will empower you in the important areas of your life.

SEE THE BIG PICTURE

The second component to seeing opportunity is the ability to identify the big picture. Several years ago, Angie was driving to a birthday party. She had specific directions to the location of the party, and about halfway to her destination, she came to a road closure. The detour was not marked very well, and Angie quickly became lost. She called me for help, and I went to a map website on my computer at work. Once she described her location, I was able to talk her through a new route to the party. As I looked at all the possibilities on the map, it was quite easy to see an alternative approach. I could see the big picture, while Angie could only see what was directly in front of her. My perspective made it very easy to see all the possibilities.

The ability to see the big picture is an art that can change the way you see everything. Every situation has a big picture, but we rarely attempt to identify it. Most people live in a perpetual tunnel, only seeing what is just ahead.

In order to begin seeing the big picture, you will need to learn how to spot and identify trends. A trend is a pattern that tends to move in a particular direction. Stock investors use trends regularly in order to determine where a stock is heading by trending price, profitability, and book value. Entrepreneurs are masters at trending, and they measure every aspect of a business to determine where things are heading. It is almost impossible to determine a company's health by looking at one single point in time. By analyzing a trend over a period of time, you can better determine where things are heading.

Virtually every component of your life is trending in one direction or another. Your marriage is improving, declining, or flat (or "trading sideways," as the financial experts like to say). Your health, your reputation at work, your relationships with your children, your relationship with God, your knowledge of a particular subject, your business, your impact on others—all are trending in some direction. If you take a period of time and simply graph whether something is better, worse, or the same over a period of time, you will start to see a trend. You can do this with anything in your life.

Whenever you analyze trends and consider the big picture, you will start to see things you've never noticed before. Or perhaps you've noticed these trends, but you've never connected the dots on why something is happening or where it is headed.

A few years after I graduated from college, I was working in a position that required very little physical exercise. As part of my job, I spent a lot of time in meetings over lunch and dinner. I was also extremely busy, so I was not working out or playing sports. Just a few years earlier, I was playing soccer, racquetball, and basketball almost daily, and I was always on the move. I had gone from large quantities of exercise and eating very little as a poor college student to *no* exercise and eating all the time. I started to have back problems, and I was tired all the time. As a result, I started drinking a lot of caffeine to compensate for my sluggish energy level.

If you had graphed my health over a five-year period, you would have spotted a very obvious trend. My health was declining due to a lack of exercise and an unhealthy diet. But at the time, I was not thinking about the big picture or the trends of my life, and I started a misguided attempt to identify solutions for my back problems. I began shopping for a new chair for my office, and Angie found a lower-back support that I installed in my company car. I researched vitamin supplements that might help.

Whenever your perspective is limited to those things immediately in front of you, you miss the obvious solutions. You are blind to the big picture. As a result, you may take shots in the dark for potential solutions, throwing as much mud against the wall as you can and hoping that something sticks.

Whenever you start to understand the trends and think big picture, you will begin to see the obvious. Instead of only seeing the symptoms, you will start to see the causes. Here's another example. Whenever I become impatient and edgy, and I find myself worrying and agonizing over situations I cannot control, there is usually a direct correlation to how my relationship with God is trending. If you were to graph my time reading the Bible and praying and see that trend declining, you would quickly start to see an impact in my life. Instead of making excuses or diagnosing the symptoms, I now use trending to clearly see the big picture and then make adjustments. This has been extremely helpful in my daily and weekly goals.

Over the next few days, I challenge you to start analyzing trends for everything you can think of and begin asking yourself what is happening in the big picture. You can do this with almost anything. Have you ever noticed how a neighborhood or a community starts to change? I've witnessed communities that suddenly started growing rapidly and others that are in decline. Think about the general population. What is happening from a trend and big-picture perspective?

I am fascinated by how technology is affecting behavior. My mom and grandmother are on Facebook and carrying iPhones, so I am starting to think about the new opportunities that may exist as a result. As you start to identify these trends, you can begin discerning what is happening in the big picture.

Once you start to see the big picture, you can start to put the method of asking effective questions to work. You can start to ask yourself: What opportunities exist as a result of these recent trends? What opportunity exists now that didn't before? What is happening in the big picture, and where is the opportunity? The art of asking the right questions, coupled with a new awareness of the big picture, will open your eyes to amazing opportunities. You will begin to see things you've never seen before.

Over time, as you practice and develop this skill, you will develop a sixth sense for opportunity. It will become second nature for you. And you will be overwhelmed at what you discover. Thomas Edison once said, "I never perfected an invention that I did not think about in terms of the service it might give others... I find out what the world needs, then I proceed to invent." Entrepreneurs have been using this skill for centuries, and now you can start using it in your personal life, in every aspect of your life.

As you apply this method of gaining perspective, you can begin identifying potential and opportunities in your spouse, your children, your friends, your career, your ministry, your hobbies, and more. You may even decide to start a new business, who knows?

You can also use the process of analyzing trends to measure your achievement in your most important goals. For example, let's say you've set a goal to have a better marriage. You and your spouse can start tracking the trend of your marriage over time. Every week, you could rate on a scale of one to ten how you are doing. After several weeks, you will start to see patterns emerge. You may find week one was an eight, week two was a seven, and week three was a five. The trend is in decline, and you need to make an adjustment. Each week, you should set a goal to do better than the last. Small, incremental changes over a period of time become massive, sustainable changes in the big picture.

It is also important to be aware of other factors that may be influencing your trends. For example, there may be a direct correlation between your marriage and your time in God's Word. There will probably be a correlation between the quality of your marriage and the consistency of your date nights together. You will soon discover that many of the important aspects of your life are all connected and related in some way or another. The value is in identifying these correlations and then making the necessary adjustments. You will discover great opportunity as your awareness of these trends fits into the big picture.

Now that you have a formula for identifying opportunity that others might miss, I encourage you to apply this process in the lives of other people as well. You can use this skill set to uncover hidden potential and opportunity in those around you. Below are a few questions that you can use:

- What are this person's two or three greatest strengths?
- How can I encourage and uncover this person's potential?
- What can I specifically do to bring value to this person?
- What potential synergies exist between this person and me? How can I nurture those synergies to reality?
- What types of opportunities exist for this person to excel?

These questions can be a starting point for uncovering great potential in those around you. You will discover a hidden treasure of opportunities in those around you, and you will have the potential to make an enormous impact. I can't even begin to describe the incredible joy that accompanies the occasion to change lives, especially in your spouse, your own children, and your friends. If you start to identify opportunities in others, you will certainly change lives, and you will dis-cover that your own life will be changed as well.

IDENTIFYING OPPORTUNITY AS A GROUP

Seeing opportunity is an exciting venture, and it is even more exciting when you are able to identify opportunities collectively as a group. Opportunity identifica-tion as a group requires a certain process, and you can use the following princi-ples to guide a group.

First, if you are leading a group, it is important that you convey the impor-tance of asking the right questions, seeing the big picture, and identifying trends. Once those elements are in practice, then you can initiate a brainstorming process that generates ideas and possibilities.

Such a brainstorming process begins with listing every conceivable idea with-out judgment. Each member of the group must be able to contribute any idea that comes to mind without fear of being criticized. Many great ideas never get to the table for fear of what others might think. As the leader of a group, you must estab-lish this environment. It is also important that once a member suggests an idea, the ownership of that particular idea transfers to the group. In many cases, people will fight for a particular idea simply because they see it as their idea. Each member must divorce himself from a particular idea once it has been given to the group.

It is imperative that every reasonable idea be listed and considered. I've found in brainstorming sessions that when a good idea has been suggested, the group will quickly abandon all other possibilities and place their focus on the one. Most of the great ideas I've ever witnessed come out of a group were usually late entries. Effective brainstorming requires that a long, good list of ideas be considered.

Once you have established a solid list of ideas, then the group should cata-log all the pros and cons of every idea. You will find that the good ideas will emerge, but here's the most important element of seeing opportunity as a group: a good idea has the potential to become a great idea when the group has the free-dom to make modifications. By asking the right questions and identifying the trends and big-picture scenario, the group will discover tweaks and changes that can be made to transform the good idea into a great idea.

SEEING OPPORTUNITY BY GOD'S DIRECTION

In this chapter so far, you have learned two components to seeing opportunity that will equip you for an amazing approach that will have an enormous impact on your life and the lives of those around you. But these two components pale in comparison to what I am about to reveal: the third component to seeing opportunity others miss is being open and listening for God's direction. I'm going to provide three examples from the Bible to illustrate the incredible potential that exists in seeing opportunity at this entirely different level.

The first example is Joseph. In chapter 2, "Creating a Climate for Change," I referenced Joseph as a man who was tethered directly to God and who possessed a solid foundation based on his relationship to God. I am amazed at Joseph's uncanny ability to see opportunity that others could not. Joseph was placed in command over all of Egypt under Pharaoh because he saw something no one else could see. Joseph warned Pharaoh that there would be seven years of abundance and then seven years of famine. As a result, grain and supplies were stockpiled during the seven years of abundance, and because of this, countless lives were saved. Joseph saw an opportunity that others could never have seen. Pharaoh placed Joseph in command because of his ability to see these things others could not see.

The second example is Moses. Moses was an amazing leader and follower of God. Moses also saw opportunity that others could not see. Moses was the man who led the Israelites out of slavery from Egypt through the parting of the Red Sea and set them on a course that would eventually lead their descendants to the Promised Land. Moses was the man who confronted Pharaoh and requested that Pharaoh release the Israelites. No one could ever have predicted how God was going to deliver the Israelites, and Moses was the one leading them at God's direction.

The third example is Paul, yet another important figure in the Bible. Paul was a zealous Pharisee, a religious leader within the Jewish tradition, who converted to Christianity in a very dramatic way. Paul was able to discern that Jesus Christ came as a sacrifice for all humankind and not just for the Jewish community. Paul recognized there was a great opportunity to preach the gospel to the Gentiles in addition to the Jews. Paul saw opportunity that most people missed.

In all three of these examples, Joseph, Moses, and Paul saw opportunity that others could never have seen. How did they do it? God revealed it to them. I referenced the big picture earlier in this chapter. The great entrepreneurs have been able to see the big picture by utilizing the skills I revealed to you, but no one can see the big picture like God can. God's perspective is beyond comprehension. He created everything, and therefore he knows everything. When you are walking in a relationship with God, you will see only what God chooses to reveal to you, but it will be what you need to see. You will have access to the only all-knowing God of the universe.

Max Lucado demonstrates this point in his book *Fearless* with the incredible story of a university student named Peter.

> Peter was a twenty-one-year-old university student when he began to experience severe pain in his right shoulder. He called his father for advice. Most students would do the same: call home for counsel. But few students have a better parent to call in such a situation. Peter's father, Michael, is a world-renowned orthopedic surgeon who specializes in shoulders. Peter calling Dr. Wirth with a shoulder problem is like Bill Gates's daughter calling him with a software question. Michael initially attributed Peter's pain to weight lifting. But after numbness and tingling set in, the doctor grew suspicious of an extremely rare shoulder condition called deep venous thrombosis. A clot was forming in his son's shoulder, dangerously close to his heart. Michael was not only acquainted with the condition; he had co-authored the paper on how to treat it. He sent Peter to the emergency room and told him to request an ultrasound. Turns out, Michael's long-distance diagnosis was right on target. Peter was immediately admitted to the hospital, where the clot was dissolved, and his earthly life was extended. Wouldn't it be great to have such a father? We do. He has diagnosed the pain of the world and written the book on its treatment. We can trust him.[7]

This example perfectly illustrates what it's like to rely on God and trust in his perfect plan. It does not get any more "big picture" than that! God has a vantage point beyond anything we can possibly imagine.

BEGIN TO SEE THINGS DIFFERENTLY

In the next few days, I challenge you to change your perspective. Begin to see things in a different light. In the movie *Dead Poets Society,* Robin Williams's character, John Keating, an English teacher at a boy's prep school, stands on top of his desk and encourages his students to join him. He asks, "Why do I stand up here?" Keating continues, "I stand upon my desk to remind myself that we must constantly look at things in a different way." If you start to ask yourself the right questions and begin to analyze important trends in order to comprehend the big picture, and if you are walking in an intimate relationship with God, I guarantee you will see things in a different way. You will begin to see opportunity that others cannot see.

CHAPTER 8

Managing Risk and Taking Action

"Do you want to be safe and good, or do you want to take a chance and be great?"

JIMMY JOHNSON, DALLAS COWBOYS COACH

Most people believe that entrepreneurialism is fairly risky. As an entrepreneur, I have been asked quite often how I became such a risk taker, as if I'm some Evel Knievel of business, throwing caution to the wind and jumping fifty buses on a motorcycle. While entrepreneurialism is not without risk, I've discovered that the great entrepreneurs are masters at minimizing risk and maximizing opportunity. They are experts at calculating the potential risk and making adjustments to minimize that risk before taking action.

I've discovered that this same ability that great entrepreneurs use to manage risk can be used in one's personal life. When I came to that realization, I really started living. I discovered that life is full of opportunities, but few are willing to capitalize on them for fear of taking a risk. Wayne Gretzky once said, "You'll always miss 100 percent of the shots you don't take."

Think about it right now. Rate yourself on a scale of one to ten. Are you really going for it, or are you holding back? I'm asking this question for every aspect of your life. Are you giving your marriage everything you've got? Are you sharing your deepest thoughts with your spouse and taking your relationship to a deeper level? Or is that too risky? What about at work—are you taking the challenging projects and putting yourself out there, or are you playing it safe? How about at church? Are you stepping up and serving in a particular ministry, or are you on the sidelines watching other people step up? How about as a parent? Are you being deliberate with your children and taking the time to truly impart knowledge and wisdom? Are you really focused on guiding them and encouraging them, or are you doing just enough to get by?

In order to really start going for it, you've got to step up and put yourself on the field, outside your zone of comfort. The real action is on the field, not on the sidelines. Great things are accomplished when you are in the game, not when you're sitting on the bench.

My freshman year in high school, I was the goalkeeper for our soccer team. About halfway through the season I broke my thumb and was not able to play for a couple of weeks, and I was scheduled to come back just a few days after an important game with one of our big rivals. I remember being relieved that I would miss that game because it was going to be tough, and I didn't want to be responsible for letting my team down. I dressed for the game, but I was not scheduled to play as I was still technically injured. I remember sitting on that bench watching the game, and then something just burned inside me. I needed to be on that field. I couldn't stand watching the battle from the sidelines and not participating. After the first quarter my team was down by one goal, and I begged the coach to put me in. After some relentless pleading, he finally decided to do so. I'm so glad that he did. I did not allow another goal the rest of the game, but more importantly, I didn't have to live in regret wondering what might have been because I wasn't willing to take the chance.

In the grand scheme of things, that was just a soccer game that no one will ever remember, but think about your everyday life for a moment. Have you taken yourself out of the game when you should be on the field? Are you taking the easy way out, sitting idle on the bench of mediocrity while life's opportunities slowly fade into regret? Have you always wondered what it would feel like to just go for it? Have you ever wondered what it would be like to just step up and be everything God created you to be? Babe Ruth once said, "Never let the fear of striking out get in your way."

In this chapter, we're going to analyze what risk is, what it means to you, and how to take calculated risks in the important areas of your life. You will be equipped to evaluate a situation and determine a course of action that minimizes failure and maximizes opportunity. You will learn to analyze when it's time to cut bait and when you should keep your line in the water. You're going to be equipped for action, and you're going to be prepared to start living your life as it ought to be lived. It's time to get off the couch and make it happen.

DEFINING RISK

Let's begin with what risk is. By most definitions, risk is the possibility of loss. Risk exists in every aspect of our lives. With every action that we take, we incur a potential risk. For example, if you decide to drive a car to the grocery store, you run the risk of getting into an accident or possibly being robbed at the store. If you take a shower, you run the risk of slipping and hurting yourself in the tub. Whenever you choose to speak to someone, you run the risk of offending them or misstating something.

You can go on forever listing every possible outcome and potential pitfall for any action that you might take. It's virtually impossible to list everything that could happen, and it's simply not practical to try to eliminate all risk. Instead, you need to balance risk with probability. Probability is the calculation of how likely something is to occur. For example, if you go to the grocery store, there is a risk that you could be robbed. However, the probability of being robbed in a grocery store in a good area is low. If you visit a grocery store in a really bad area where people are robbed on a regular basis, then the probability of getting robbed at that store might be much higher.

Many people fall into two different categories as it relates to risk. The first category includes those who will take a chance without analyzing anything. I call this the *blind man jumping* group. The second category includes those who are unwilling to take any risk at all. We'll call this group the *recluse turtles*.

BLIND MAN JUMPING

The blind man jumping group will make a decision and simultaneously ignore anything about it that could be perceived as negative. They close their eyes to the possibility of a downside, and they move forward with an incomplete picture of how things are. This approach can be very dangerous. I've encountered those who will take 5 percent of the information they need and make a 100 percent decision in a matter of a few moments.

A person who is unwilling to acknowledge or consider the pitfalls of a potential action or decision will eventually run headfirst into disaster. Imagine starting a business with your house as collateral for a business loan—and you've not considered the risk of the venture. Your unwillingness to acknowledge potential downsides could lead to financial ruin. Imagine dating someone and making the decision to get married in a month. Envision taking a new job in another state without considering all the possibilities.

I've listened to people from the blind man jumping group defend their unwillingness to acknowledge potential pitfalls as having an optimistic outlook. I've heard things like, "You have to throw caution to the wind and go for it if you expect to succeed." That type of thinking can be dangerous. I've witnessed others who have made big purchases (car, house, etc.) without really thinking through their financial situation or the stability of their future income.

THE RECLUSE TURTLES

On the other side of the spectrum, there are many who never step out and take action because they *only* see the potential downside. The recluse turtles are unwilling to accept risk. They are paralyzed by fear, and they will never open themselves to the possibility of any real opportunity. Recluse turtles live in a constant risk-avoidance mentality.

Some recluse turtles don't even realize they are avoiding risk. They enjoy dreaming about the possibilities of adventure and opportunity, and yet they will never take a chance on anything. You probably know some people like this. They love to talk about their dreams and aspirations, but they rarely, if ever, take action.

Think for a moment about which end of the spectrum you lean toward. Are you a blind man jumping, or are you a recluse turtle? Your inclination toward one end over the other will usually dictate how you view probability. If you are a recluse turtle, then you assume the probability of being robbed in the grocery store in a good area is higher than it actually is. If you are a blind man jumping, then you could never imagine being robbed. It is unlikely that you are on one extreme end or the other, but you probably do lean in a particular direction as it relates to risk. It is important that you know this about yourself. The more you are aware of your own tendencies, the more effective you will become in risk analysis and making effective decisions.

RISK VERSUS REWARD

Another important component to evaluating risk is the relationship between risk and reward. Many people mistakenly equate risk with chance or luck. They assume that the greater the risks you are willing to take, the greater the reward you will receive. Some believe the great entrepreneurs became great through the luck of the draw, the roll of the dice. They have created a false connection between risk and reward. Do not assume that just because the risk is high the reward will also be high. While this correlation can exist in some cases, it does not exist in all situations.

Managing Risk and Taking Action
121

As you learn the process for managing risk, you will discover that it is possible to take a course of action that is low in risk and high in reward. You need to adopt a new paradigm for considering risk. Taking a risk should never be equated with being hasty or reckless. General George Patton once said, "Take calculated risks. That is quite different from being rash."

In the pages that follow, I'm going to outline five steps to managing risk in your personal life. You will be equipped to calculate risk, minimize the downside, and start taking action by maximizing your best opportunities.

FIVE STEPS TO MANAGING RISK

Step 1: Get the Specifics. The process for analyzing risk begins first with information. You must have information, and you will need specifics. If you lean toward the blind man jumping group, you probably think you only need 5 percent of the available information to make a decision. Don't fall into the trap of researching too little.

I recently met with someone who was considering a career change. This person was contemplating a job offer in a completely different industry. It was certainly a risk, and he was trying to determine if it made sense to make the change. He would be taking a cut in pay, but he thought there would be a lot more upside potential in the future in this particular industry versus the one he was currently working in. I asked him several questions, and I quickly concluded that he did not have enough information. He didn't know what the average salary was for the industry. He didn't know what the job description was, and he had very little information on the company he would be working for. I concluded that it was not possible to make a good decision with the limited information he had. Warren Buffett once said, "Risk comes from not knowing what you're doing."

Before you can analyze and evaluate a potential decision, you need to get the specifics. If you lean toward the recluse turtle group, then you probably think you need 100 percent of the available information in order to make a decision. The problem with this mentality is that it might take a lifetime to collect 100 percent of the information! I have found that it is usually possible to collect 70 to 80 percent of the available information in a reasonable amount of time, and you can do an appropriate risk analysis with that amount of information.

As you collect your information, remember that you must understand the details, and you should be able to clearly communicate those details to others. If you are unable to explain your position and plans in a coherent manner to others, then one of the three scenarios exist:

- You really do not have all the information you need to make a decision.
- The decision or plan you are preparing to make is not a good one.
- You did not do a good job of explaining your position. If you were merely ineffective in communicating your position, then try again until they do understand. If you are *unable* to clearly and logically delineate your reasoning to others, then you probably do not have all the information or your plan is not a good one.

I am amazed at how often people have shared a game plan or approach with me without really understanding all the details. A few years ago, I was in discussions with some potential partners on a business opportunity. I sat in a meeting as they described their plan. Everyone in the room nodded in agreement as they talked through all the details, but I just did not understand the plan. I'm usually not the smartest guy in a room, but I finally decided to reveal my ignorance, and I said, "I have no idea how this is really going to work. Can you explain how this is really going to work?"

Before I could finish my question, all the other potential partners around the table agreed with my sentiment. In fact, one person said, "Thank you. I thought I was the only one." The amazing thing is that people are often afraid to look foolish by revealing their lack of understanding, so they'll keep silent instead of getting the information they need. I have learned that it is better to ask the tough questions, because if you do not understand, there is probably a reason.

As you collect your information and evaluate the details, never be afraid to ask with boldness. Ask again and again until you truly understand.

Step 2: Be Realistic and Objective. One critical element to evaluating a potential decision is the ability to be realistic and objective. If you are faced with a particular decision, you must separate yourself from any strong emotional ties you may have to a certain direction. For example, if you are contemplating buying a new home, it can be very easy to become emotionally invested. You might overlook negative details and warning signs because of your feelings. Many people have made terrible financial decisions by buying a new home they could not afford because they were emotionally invested.

One way to remain objective is to solicit advice and assistance from someone who is not personally involved in your particular decision. Often an unbiased person can provide the perspective that is needed, and he or she can offer insight you may have missed. I've discovered that many people have a reluctance to ask for feedback from someone who doesn't share their point of view. Never back away from collecting such feedback. If someone shares a dissenting opinion from your own, take the time to ask why. Whenever someone disagrees with me, I want to know why, and I want them to explain their reasoning. You will be amazed at the valuable information you can collect and what you may learn from people who see things differently than you do.

Step 3: Play Devil's Advocate. This component is extremely important. If you are considering a particular approach, then you should take that approach and try to poke as many holes in it as you possibly can. You should solicit help in this area from an unbiased person, as he or she will see things you will inevitably miss. It is particularly important that you consider potential pitfalls and downsides before making a final decision.

Step 4: Modify the Approach. As you begin to uncover flaws and holes in your particular approach, you can begin to make improvements and adjustments. This is the secret sauce of minimizing risk.

Several years ago, my business partner, Lonnie, and I had an idea for a sales training seminar. We recognized a gap in the market for sales training that would be based on personality styles.

As we considered this opportunity, we created a business plan that included a lot of information and specifics. Our initial plan called for sales training seminars that would be conducted for an entire week in major metropolitan cities across the US. At first, it seemed like a great idea. We knew there was a need for this type of training, and there was limited competition. On the surface, it appeared to be the perfect idea.

We could have taken that idea and charged headfirst into a new business, unwilling to also consider the potential pitfalls and downsides. The result would probably have been a failed business venture. Instead, we worked tirelessly to analyze the likely outcomes.

We have always used the following philosophy: If we have an idea, throw it on the whiteboard and start shooting holes in it. If it's a great idea, it will hold up under the scrutiny. If it's a good idea with holes, then we'll figure out where the holes are and patch them, thus transforming the good idea into a great idea. If it's not that good of an idea, it will crash and burn under our attack.

I'd rather have an idea crash and burn on the whiteboard in my office than in the real world with my money behind it. Wouldn't you agree?

We put our idea of weeklong personality-based sales training seminars on the whiteboard. As we started to analyze every possible pitfall and downside we could think of, it became clear that our business model would only generate a small profit—with above-average risk. The numbers just did not work. In fact, we started to look at other companies that were offering similar services, and they were struggling financially. We had to decide if the entire idea should be scrapped or if there was another alternative.

After a few more days of consideration, we came up with a new model. We realized that a one-day or half-day training at a much lower cost would be more palatable for small businesses. A small business could afford to send its sales staff for a training seminar that only lasted four to eight hours rather than a full week. We also believed that we could produce accelerated content with leave-behind materials for self-study once the training was complete.

The result of our new alternative was a business model that produced tenfold more potential profit. We did not eliminate the risk completely, but our analysis and assessment minimized the downside and dramatically improved the potential upside.

A fair assessment of both sides of a potential decision will not always equate into a go/no-go decision. It's not always all or nothing. In many cases, there's an alternative approach that exists, but you have to be willing to work through the process of assessing the risk and benefit in order to identify this alternative. The process of modifying your approach is where risk is minimized, and it is also where opportunities can be maximized.

Step 5: Evaluate the Probability. In every decision you make, there will be a potential upside and a potential downside, and there will be a probability for each. I have discovered that the following ten questions can be invaluable in assessing whether to move forward or not and in determining the risk and probability:

- What is the best-case scenario if I move forward?
- What is the probability that the best-case scenario will become reality?
- What is the realistic and likely outcome if things go well in this approach?
- What is the worst-case scenario if I move forward?
- What is the probability that the worst-case scenario will become reality?
- Can I live with the results of the worst-case scenario?
- What is the realistic, likely outcome if things do not go well in this approach?

- If I move forward with this decision, and I later discover the worst-case scenario is likely, what action can I take to avert and/or minimize the worst-case scenario?
- What is the risk if I choose not to move forward?
- What regrets may I have if I do not move forward?

I have often discovered that my worst-case scenario is not as probable as I initially thought. I have also learned that in many cases, the risk of not taking action was much greater for me than the risk of taking action. The purpose of these questions is to force you to really analyze the situation and weigh the potential outcomes. You will find that your ability to become more decisive and deliberate will increase exponentially once you put this approach into practice.

It is true that in rare cases you may end up in a worst-case scenario, and it is important that you think about that particular result and how you will deal with it. You have to ponder question six: can you live with it?

Question eight is designed to inspire a ripcord strategy. The ripcord strategy is a last-resort measure that you should only employ if your worst-case scenario begins to play out. In many cases, if you have planned appropriately in advance, you can use a ripcord strategy to minimize the results of a worst-case scenario. It is helpful if this strategy is in place in advance of taking action. Among other things, preplanning will help you know when is it time to eject well in advance so that you do not give up on an opportunity prematurely when you are overwhelmed with emotion in the heat of the moment.

As an example, when I started my first business, I calculated all the risks, and I estimated a worst-case scenario in addition to devising a ripcord strategy. I don't want to give you the wrong idea: you should never go into a situation with the thought of retreat at the front of your mind. That said, it is important to consider all implications in advance and make preparations. Before I quit my full-time job to start my first business, I calculated exactly how long I could survive on my savings. I then estimated how long I would need to find a new job if the business failed, and then I came to a number of months that I could go before it was time to pull the ripcord. Each month that we made money, I extended the number of months I could survive.

I never planned on failure, and I had a lot on the line when I started that business, but I also had a strategy in case my worst-case scenario played out. I estimated the probability as low, but I still made the necessary preparations just in case. I found that when the tough times came, and they certainly came, I never worried about whether to abandon my strategy. That decision had already been made before I began.

Another example of a ripcord strategy might be in the context of a decision to serve in an area where you've never served before. Maybe you are considering the opportunity to serve in your church as a preschool Sunday school teacher. In that situation, I would put a time frame on your initial commitment and communicate that time frame up front. You may find that you are better suited for working with high-school students than you are with preschool students, but you will only know after you give it a try. You may decide to serve as a preschool Sunday school teacher for three months as a trial to gauge whether that is the best decision. If you put that timeline in place, you will be less likely to bail out in the first week if things do not go well. This will prevent you from making an emotional decision in the heat of the moment, and it will also provide an exit strategy for you if you determine you're serving in the wrong area.

In many cases, a ripcord strategy is similar to disaster planning and emergency preparedness, but there are some areas of your life where a ripcord strategy should never be considered and can actually be detrimental to your situation. Marriage, for example, should never have a ripcord strategy. When you decide to make the commitment of marriage, you are committing for better or for worse. Parenting is another example. When you become a parent, you are a parent for the rest of your child's life. No ripcord strategies on that one. The same goes for your relationship with God. Any kind of ripcord strategies in these areas will do more damage than good.

As you work through these five steps of managing risk, you will begin to create the confidence to start taking action in the important areas of your life. I want to encourage you to think about your future actions as if they are future investments. As an investor, you should always be focused on achieving a good return on investment. Your actions, time, and money are all investments. Do not waste any of those resources on opportunities that will not produce returns. Make investments in the most important areas of your life. You should know exactly what those areas are at this point in this book. Make investments that will last for an eternity.

ELIMINATE RISK BY BEING AT THE CENTER OF GOD'S WILL

There is one final area of risk to address, and this is a complete game-changer. If you are in an intimate, active relationship with God, there will be times when God will call you to do something that may appear very risky, even crazy. At first glance, the recluse turtle in you will want to get out of the game, onto the sidelines where things appear to be safe. In reality, there is only one safe place that exists in the entire world—the center of God's will. It may not always seem that way, but I assure you that it is! You put yourself in extreme risk whenever you remove yourself from the center of God's will and whenever your focus is not on God.

One night, Jesus's disciples went out on a boat, and it was struggling along against the wind and waves. Dawn was quickly approaching, and the disciples saw a man out walking on the water. At first they were terrified and thought it was a ghost, but Jesus said to them, "Take courage! It is I. Don't be afraid." As miraculous as this must have been to the disciples (and to us, for that matter), this was not a big deal for Jesus. He created all things including the water, so walking on it was not a big deal. But I am amazed at what Peter did after realizing it was Jesus walking on the water. In an incredible act of boldness, Peter said to Jesus, "Lord, if it's you, tell me to come to you on the water."[1]

I still can't believe Peter asked to do this, and I wonder what the other disciples thought at that moment. This was certainly an incredible opportunity. How many people get the chance to walk on water? Peter, with all his shortcomings, had the boldness to ask for this opportunity. On another occasion Jesus said, "You may ask me for anything in my name, and I will do it."[2] It is important to note that God wants us to ask him and rely on him. He will give us anything as long as it is in the confines of his will.

After Peter asked to walk on the water, Jesus responded with one word: "Come."[3] I guarantee you that you are surrounded by opportunities to do something very similar to what Peter did. You currently have opportunities to step out in faith and do great things. You have the opportunity to be an exceptional husband or wife, father or mother, brother or sister, son or daughter, friend, pastor, teacher, boss, employee, leader, follower, and so on. You are surrounded by opportunities to step up and take a chance. Incredible adventures await you at this very moment. If you are asking God right now for these opportunities, and they are in his will, then he may be calling you right now to step out of the boat and onto the water. He may be holding his hand out at this very moment and saying to you, "Come."

After Jesus told Peter to come, Peter did something many of us fail to do. Peter got out of the boat and onto the water, and he started toward Jesus. What an incredible feeling that must have been! But after Peter started toward Jesus, something happened—Peter saw the wind and became afraid. Peter took his eyes off of Jesus, and he started to sink.

Take a moment and reflect on this question: what is God speaking to you about right now?

Jesus could easily have calmed the wind and provided a perfectly smooth lake for Peter to make his first water-walk on. He is God, after all. He could have snapped a finger and created the perfect conditions, but he did not. He doesn't do that with us either, because he is all we need. Peter started to sink because he took his focus off Jesus. It had nothing to do with the wind and waves.

As Peter started to sink, he cried out, "Lord, save me!"[4] Jesus immediately caught him and rescued him. Your greatest risk-mitigation plan possible, and your greatest strategy for maximizing opportunities, must include a consistent and intimate relationship with God. The circumstances that surround you, however bleak they may appear, will have no effect on you when you are completely focused on God and at the center of his will.

I encourage you now to take action on those things you've been hiding from. Get off the bench, and put yourself in the game. You can never imagine the amazing things you will accomplish until you take a chance and step up.[5]

CHAPTER 9

The Work Ethic

"I firmly believe that any man's finest hour, the greatest fulfillment of all that he holds dear, is that moment when he has worked his heart out in a good cause and lies exhausted on the field of battle—victorious."

VINCE LOMBARDI

I absolutely love bow hunting. Over the years I have spent many trips hunting with my father-in-law, and I have always treasured the opportunities to escape everything and be virtually alone in the woods. I love everything about it, and Angie can attest to my passion for the sport. It usually begins for me around March or April. I record all the outdoor hunting specials on television, and I find myself inserting hunting stories in my everyday conversations.

Angie is a saint to tolerate my obsessive behavior, but I cannot help myself. I discuss the topic with people who probably don't enjoy or understand hunting that much. I have several hunting friends at church, and every Sunday, we remind ourselves of the number of days left before bow season begins.

As the season draws closer, I research and scout the areas I plan to hunt, and I spend a considerable amount of effort and time surveying and preparing.

In order to achieve any level of success in deer hunting, you must understand the patterns of the deer, the lay of the land, and appropriate stand placement for bow shots. This takes a great deal of time and effort, especially during the summer months when the temperatures are above ninety degrees. During this preparation time, I will clear trees, debris, and sometimes large tree limbs in order to erect and place tree stands in the perfect locations. I also spend a lot of time on target practice.

Several years ago on the morning of opening day of bow season, I rose at 3 a.m., trying my best not to wake my sleeping wife and children. I took my shower using scent-free soaps and deodorant, and I dressed myself in full camouflage. All my clothing had been washed with special scent-free detergents. (This is the one time of the year I can be found putting clothes in the washing machine in my

129

home.) I quietly slipped out of the house and into the truck, and my father-in-law and I traveled for an hour and a half to our hunting location.

I recall packing my bags, preparing my bow, checking the flashlight batteries, and performing hundreds of other small tasks in order to be completely prepared. I sprayed myself down with scent blocker, and we walked for what seemed an eternity to the location where I would be hunting. I remember taking each step in great anticipation for what I might see that morning. My heart was pounding as if I had been running a marathon. Surprisingly, I was not tired, despite my lack of sleep for weeks leading up to this hunt. I spent great care to be as quiet as possible as I worked a climber stand into a tree I had scouted months earlier. After getting the stand positioned in the tree, I hoisted my bow from the ground, and finally I could take a breath, sit down, and relax.

I absolutely savor those moments, the moment I am able to just relax in the stand and wait and think. I am alone with my thoughts and God without any distractions. I find that my mind is clear and my anxiety slowly fades. I am at peace, and simultaneously I wait in great anticipation for what might walk down my path.

On that particular morning, for some strange reason, I asked myself this question: "Why do I love bow hunting so much when it requires such hard work?" I had never asked the question before, and I wasn't asking the question because I was growing weary of hunting or of the process that's required. I asked it out of pure curiosity. Why *did* I love hunting so much when it required such work and effort?

Later that day, I met with my father-in-law over lunch back at camp, and I posed the question to him. He thought for several moments, and then a smile came to his face as he finally concluded, "Anything that is worthwhile requires hard work." I initially accepted his answer as a token response without giving much thought to it, but as I slowly walked back to my stand that afternoon, it hit me. *He's got it, that's exactly the answer*, I thought. Anything that is worthwhile requires hard work (aside from salvation). I thought of everything that has ever meant anything to me in my life, and then I recalled what it required of me. This is a principle that holds true: Anything that is worthwhile requires hard work.

Can you think of anything in your life that is of any value that does not require some level of effort from you? Consider any achievement, goal, skill, relationship, marriage, friend, child, education, career. In most cases, I would argue that the things you treasure most require the most from you.

The great entrepreneurs understand this principle, and they put it into practice every day. A strong work ethic is the engine of success. People who have limited potential, mediocre skills, and average talent can achieve amazing things when they employ a strong work ethic. It is a game-changer. This one component has the potential to increase your effectiveness and accomplishments exponentially, and yet it is the most overlooked and underestimated quality of successful people.

I am amazed at the number of people who come to the United States with virtually nothing but the shirts on their backs, with limited skills, education, money, and ability to communicate, and yet they achieve unbelievable things. Most people who were not born into abundance recognize that you must work hard to achieve great things. Talent, ability, and money are completely useless in the absence of hard work.

The Bible says, "Those who work their land will have abundant food, but those who chase fantasies have no sense"; "Diligent hands will rule, but laziness ends in forced labor"; "Lazy hands make for poverty, but diligent hands bring wealth."[1] A strong work ethic is one of the best-kept and most overlooked secrets to success.

If you could take your talents, abilities, and skills and roll them up into a number that reflected your overall potential, you could use that number to compare your potential to someone else's potential. But that number would be of no value in reality, because it is affected by a person's work ethic. The work ethic acts as a multiplier. Your decision to work hard or be lazy has a multiplying effect on your potential in a positive or negative way.

You had no control over the talents and abilities you were born with, but there is one thing you do have control over: the amount of effort you decide to exert in the employment of those talents and abilities. That's completely controlled by you. It is in your hands, and you decide every day what you will do with it. Thomas Edison once said, "Opportunity is missed by most people because it is dressed in overalls and looks like work."

Every successful entrepreneur I have ever met or interacted with had a strong work ethic. I discovered when I started my first business that it would not be possible to sit back in an office and expect the checks to start rolling in. It doesn't work that way.

I remember my first day on a new job at Johnson & Johnson, and I recall feeling overwhelmed that I did not have the background to do the job. My education was specific to business and very light in science, and yet I was required to possess a strong knowledge of the products I was to sell. I'll never forget one of the key vice presidents sharing his tips for success in the job: "There is no replacement for hard work and common sense." I took those words to heart, and I made sure that I worked harder than anyone on my team to compensate for the lack of science in my background.

It's amazing that those individuals who commit themselves to extraordinary effort and hard work will in most cases accomplish more than those who are far more talented, educated, and experienced but do not put forth the same amount of effort.

If the idea of work ethic is foreign or frightening to you, hold on. In the remainder of this chapter, you are going to learn a new perspective on hard work. I am going to outline a process for reprogramming the way you think about hard work and demonstrate what the great entrepreneurs already know and use every day. You are going to learn how to accelerate your potential and ultimate success, and you will begin to see immediate benefits in your relationship to God, your marriage, your relationships with others, your effectiveness, and your own contentment.

Many people in the world today do just enough to get by. They seek out the easy course, taking the path of least resistance. They perceive hard work and effort from a shortsighted perspective, and they lose sight of the rewards that come later. They find that the pain of hard work far outweighs the gain of the future result, and they fail to connect the longer-term pain that is associated with a lack of effort. Zig Ziglar says, "When you are tough on yourself, life is inevitably easy. When you are easy on yourself, life will be inevitably difficult."

Pain Versus Gain

Let's first examine why most people choose to take the path of least resistance. This mindset is formulated by how you view immediate benefit versus future benefit and immediate pain versus future pain. An individual who has a difficult time putting forth effort or getting motivated and working hard will typically view immediate work or effort as painful, without considering the future benefit of the work. This type of person can be so shortsighted as to only see the pain of the hard work without the future gain.

Shortly after I was married and working a full-time job, I began gaining some weight. I couldn't climb more than two flights of stairs without gasping for air. I had reached a point in my life when my physical activity was at a minimum, and I was eating a square four meals per day with lots of Hostess and Little Debbie's mixed in between.

I decided it was time to start jogging. I'll never forget the very first time I hit the pavement and ventured around the block in my neighborhood. I was completely out of shape, and it was a miserable experience. As a shortsighted person at that time, I remember telling myself that I would never do that again. Why should I? It was hard work, miserable, and hot, and I was feeling pain.

A few weeks after my first attempt at jogging, I had the great privilege of seeing Zig Ziglar speak at a convention. Zig spoke about pain, and he shared that his philosophy used to be, "If you are going to experience good health, you have to pay the price." Zig would always repeat the line "pay the price" for anything that you might work for in your life.

He later realized that you don't pay the price for good health by working out and eating properly, but you do pay the price if you *don't* choose to work out and eat healthy. You ultimately pay the price if you don't choose to set a goal and seek to achieve it.

I later thought about my failed attempt at jogging, and I decided I was now paying the price for not working on good health. I finally made the connection that the longer-term gain of good health far outweighed the short-term pain of working out.

THREE STEPS TO CREATING A STRONG WORK ETHIC

Step 1: Identify the Long-Term Gain. The first step in changing your work ethic is building your awareness of all the good consequences (or long-term gains) that will be achieved for the pain you endure in the short term. This is called the pain/gain principle, and it has to do with how you see pain and gain in your daily actions. The great entrepreneurs see the long-term gain almost intuitively, because the whole purpose of starting a new business is to grow it into something that does not exist in the beginning. The very nature of entrepreneurialism forces you to focus on the future benefit. But the average person rarely thinks in this way. The average person is usually more focused on the short-term pain of a particular action.

The best example of the pain/gain principle is revealed in *The Stanford Marshmallow Study*. Michael Mischel, a Stanford psychology researcher, performed a study that began in the 1960s with four-year-olds and marshmallows. Four-year-old children were given one marshmallow. Did I mention that these children were also very hungry? The children were given two options. They could eat the one marshmallow now, or if they waited for fifteen or so minutes until the researcher returned, they could have a second marshmallow—but only if they did not eat the first one.

This study revealed some very interesting results. About one third of the children devoured the marshmallow as soon as the researcher left the room. Other children were able to wait a little longer before succumbing to the pressure. The remaining one third of the children waited fifteen minutes or longer until the researcher returned without eating their one marshmallow.

The long-term results of this study are very telling. The children who were able to view the long-term gain of two marshmallows while enduring the immediate pain of not eating the one marshmallow in front of them in the heat of the moment went on to experience a greater amount of success in their lives. After the children graduated high school, the group that had waited for the second marshmallow was more positive, self-motivating, and persistent in the face of trials. These children had the habits of successful people, and those habits translated into better health, higher salaries, and better marriages.[2]

The pain/gain principle can yield amazing results in your life if you can start to delay instant gratification and focus on the long-term gain that can be achieved. If you choose to take the path of least resistance, you are setting yourself up on a course for failure and misery. This principle affects your career, your spiritual walk with God, your marriage, your health, your role as a parent, your education, and anything else that is important to you.

For example, there are many times when children need to be disciplined. Sometimes parents don't feel like going through the trouble that is required to discipline them. It's easier to just ignore their children's behavior or send them to their rooms with a Nintendo DS in hand. The short-term pain of going through the process of disciplining children is sometimes greater in the mind of a parent than the long-term pain of dealing with spoiled children in the future. The even longer-term pain to consider is how those spoiled children will turn out when they reach adulthood. It is imperative that parents recognize the long-term gain of guiding their children into responsible adulthood as the benefit for dealing with the immediate pain of disciplining their children in the present.

Another example is education. If you endure the short-term pain of going to school, studying hard, and taking tests to complete a degree, then you avoid the long-term pain of working in a job that pays less with limited opportunities for advancement. The path of least resistance would dictate that you skip college, because attending college requires effort and hard work, or pain in the short term. However, the students who do endure the pain of hard work and effort in attending classes and taking tests will reap the rewards or long-term gain after they have graduated.

If you are struggling to take action on something you know to be important, the reason you are hesitating is most likely that you identify more pain with taking the action than with not taking the action.

The great entrepreneurs are excellent at taking action on their most important priorities because they are focused on the long-term gain. You need to begin thinking in this same way.

Step 2: Change Your Expectations. The second step to changing your work ethic is to change your expectations. Most people today expect very little of themselves and therefore achieve very little. Never settle for mediocrity when you can have so much more! A strong work ethic is a mindset, and it will take work and effort to develop it. You must raise the bar of expectations for yourself in every aspect of your life.

One powerful way to raise your expectations is to surround yourself with hardworking, motivated people. When I started working for Johnson & Johnson, I found myself working with several extremely talented and hardworking people. It was during that time in my life that I realized I had the potential to do so much more.

One of my coworkers and I became good friends over a period of time, and we decided together that we would like to enter the technology industry. We were initially just dreaming of such a leap, considering that neither one of us had any technology experience or background in the industry.

After a good deal of research, we decided to seek out some certifications that would help us to enter the industry. The particular certification we were interested in required six exams that were closely tied to some training courses, and those courses were very expensive. At this point, most people just dream of making the next step—very few ever take the challenge of overcoming their first obstacle. I used to thoroughly enjoy the concept of dreaming about making changes and taking on new challenges, but I very rarely did the actual work to achieve it. I usually told everyone around me what I was planning to do, but unfortunately, I came up short with sharing the successes. The Bible says, "All hard work brings a profit, but mere talk leads only to poverty."[3]

A few weeks after discovering the cost of the training and the work required to achieve this goal, I had decided to retire this dream for a new one. It was then that my friend completely shocked me. He had purchased several books that covered the necessary material for the first exam. He studied day and night for two weeks while I was out talking about it!

After all his hard work, my friend passed his first certification exam. The next day we met for lunch, and he proudly displayed his results. I couldn't believe it. I had never considered the possibility of studying at home, nor had I considered the actual work of studying in general to accomplish such a task.

Later that evening, I decided I would also self-study and pass every exam needed to complete the certification. Within four months, we had passed all six certifications, and we were both working in the technology industry. I am even proud to say that I passed my last exam to complete the certification before my friend passed his. I can't stress enough the importance of surrounding yourself with motivated, hardworking people. This paradigm shift literally changed the course of my life and career.

Another component to your expectations of yourself has to do with your own beliefs about what is required of you. Sometimes we underestimate what it will take in terms of effort to accomplish a particular goal. You have to be realistic about what is required, or you will end up with a workload that exceeds your availability. You will also become very frustrated if your expectations don't match what's required.

My oldest son, Wyatt, and I started taking karate a few years ago. On our first night, we received a karate uniform and a white belt. Wyatt quickly noticed that others had different colored belts based on their progress and achievement. We received the white belts for showing up, but you had to work for the remaining belts.

Wyatt found out that the yellow belt was the first belt, and he decided he wanted it, but he didn't realize the amount of work that would be required. His expectations weren't even close to reality. He just assumed that after a few weeks of attending classes, he should get his yellow belt.

I want to encourage you now to analyze your own expectations about the things you are working on. Are your expectations realistic and in line with what's required? There are many who start their first job and think they should be in management in less than a year. There are others in school who think they deserve a passing grade just because they attended all the lectures. Our society has adopted an entitlement philosophy. You should get the trophy whether you win or lose. If you show up, you get the prize. But life doesn't work that way. You have to accurately assess what's required and then commit yourself to working diligently for it.

Wyatt eventually came to the understanding of what he needed to do to earn his yellow belt. We both worked every night on the skills and techniques we needed to master. After several months of hard work, we both tested and were awarded our yellow belts.

I can't begin to describe the sense of pride written all over Wyatt the night he received his yellow belt. This wasn't just something he got for showing up. He had worked hard and earned it, and he knew it. There's an incredible feeling of accomplishment that comes with a job well done. Wyatt would have never understood the great satisfaction of accomplishment had he just received his yellow belt for showing up every night.

You should have a sense of pride and excellence in everything that you do, even in the mundane. There should be no job too small or unimportant for you not to give it your best. Martin Luther King, Jr., once said, "If a man is called to be a street cleaner, he should sweep the streets even as Michelangelo painted or Beethoven composed music or Shakespeare wrote poetry. He should sweep the streets so well that all the hosts of heaven will pause to say, here lived a great street sweeper who did his job so well."

Consider your potential for just a moment. God designed you with a specific purpose in mind, and he gave you a wealth of resources and gifts. Those resources don't amount to anything if you are not willing to support them with hard work and determination. A strong work ethic will also have a direct correlation to your success in your career.

I currently own and manage several businesses. In those businesses, we sometimes hire people with a lot of education and multiple technical degrees, and at other times, we look for people with a high-school-level education. Each job has a different set of requirements in terms of education, experience, and so on, but there is one common denominator that is essential for hiring employees in any organization that I own: a strong work ethic.

Companies and organizations today would give anything to hire employees who maintain a strong work ethic. Many key managers have shared that they will hire extremely talented, educated, experienced individuals, only to find within a few months that these employees do not have a strong work ethic. That discovery will ultimately lead to termination at some point in the future.

Another important component to changing your expectations is the mental endurance you create over time. When you step up and take on a whole new level in your work ethic, your mental and physical endurance may not be at an optimal level. But just like exercise, if you continue, your mind and body will soon adapt, and you will perform at that new level with command and ease.

I remember my first semester my freshman year in college. I'll never forget the culture shock that first week when my instructors provided the workload requirements for my respective courses. I recall thinking that college was too much work, and I was quickly wishing I had never left high school. It is interesting that after my first semester, I adapted and soon concluded that college wasn't that difficult. My expectations adjusted, and I began performing at a whole new level.

I now wonder what my grade-point average might have been in high school if I had studied as hard there as I did in college. I am sure I would be amazed at my grade-point average in college if I had worked as hard as I do now! Don't be afraid of stepping up your expectations as it relates to your work ethic. You will be amazed at what you can achieve.

When I began jogging again, the first few weeks were complete torture for me, but soon I was jogging over five miles at a time. I no longer considered jogging to be torture when I allowed my body and mind to adjust to a new level, and I set new expectations for what was possible.

Step 3: Confirm that Your Effort Matches Your Priorities. It is extremely important that your work ethic match your most important priorities. Unfortunately, there are many people who do maintain a strong work ethic in certain areas of their lives, but they compartmentalize this ethic into the areas that aren't of highest priority. Let me be extremely clear that a strong work ethic should apply to every aspect of your life in balance, because some of you who are reading this right now are feeling justified by having a strong work ethic in your career only. There is a great danger for those who choose to immerse themselves in a career or hobby while simultaneously ignoring other aspects of their lives.

Beth Moore once said something regarding this topic that changed my entire life. She said, "No amount of success outside the home can ever make up for a failure within the home." Isn't that true? There are countless so-called successful people in our society today who have achieved greatness in their respective careers—sports, business, writing, investing, politics—but the reality is that they have destroyed their personal lives in the process.

What difference does it make if you achieve great success outside the home, but you reach the end of your life to find that you failed miserably as a husband or wife, father or mother, friend or Christian?

The problem for those individuals who have put all their energy into just one area of their lives is that they have forfeited their top priorities unknowingly. Many people have a false paradigm that says they must sacrifice everything else in their lives in order to be great in one area. It's a shame that anyone would live by such a self-limiting philosophy.

A strong work ethic applies to much more than a career, education, or professional achievement. Those things are all important, but we must strive for a strong work ethic in every aspect of our lives, including but not limited to our relationship with Jesus Christ, our marriages, parenting, friendship, our health, our finances, and our charity and compassion to those who need it.

Why be great in your career if you are only mediocre as a parent? Why choose to be a great politician if you end up failing in your marriage? A strong work ethic is a mindset, a paradigm about how we live every aspect and dimension of our lives.

The benefits of a strong work ethic in a marriage can be the difference between success and failure in that marriage. A husband and wife who both work hard at their marriage will be more likely to respect each other and care for each other. Marriage is extremely hard work. It does not just happen on its own. Mike Huckabee once said, "Marriage is not a 50/50 venture, but it is a 100/100 venture."

If you want to be in outstanding physical condition, you have to be willing to hit the gym, eat correctly, take vitamins, and avoid junk food. If you want to have an outstanding marriage, you have to be willing to work hard in the marriage by sacrificing, loving when it's not easy to love, and placing your spouse's needs above your own. Likewise, raising small children requires an enormous amount of effort and work, and it takes both spouses to step up and work hard to make their marriage and family a success. The expectations that you once had about your role in a marriage may prove to be grossly underestimated upon the arrival of your first child.

The expectations that we set for ourselves will affect how we live and how hard we will work in the different areas of our lives. Many people never have the expectation of a great marriage. They have seen many people struggle in their marriages, so they proceed into a marriage with the expectation of mediocrity. Many people never expect to be outstanding parents with deep, loving relationships with their children, especially if they didn't have similar experiences in their own childhood. I'm encouraging you right now to change those expectations for yourself. You have the ability to be great in all the important areas of your life.

Perhaps the most important area of hard work is your personal walk with the Lord. Consider this the most important relationship in your life. I believe

Christians today may find themselves very hard at work with their career, family, education, ministries, and hobbies, but very few are committed to working extremely hard in their relationship with Jesus Christ. I want you to get excited about a whole new standard you could be setting in your life today, here, at this very moment.

I was asked once in a seminar, "If there was one thing you could do consistently well that would have the greatest impact on your life, what would it be?" I pondered the question, and I considered what that one thing would be. What if I could be the greatest husband to my wife? What if I could be the best father I could possibly be? What if I could communicate flawlessly? What if I could be an outstanding entrepreneur? What if I could encourage other people? And then it struck me: what if I could have an outstanding relationship with Jesus Christ, the Creator and Savior of my very soul and life? What kind of impact would that have on me as a husband, father, son, friend, coworker, author, and teacher?

I carefully considered the impact of being in an intimate relationship with the Living Lord of Universe. Would it influence my decision-making? Would it completely fulfill my purpose in life? I concluded that I must work harder than anything to ensure my relationship with the Lord was the first priority in my life.

Take a moment now to answer this question for yourself. If there was one thing you could do consistently well that would have the greatest impact on your life, what would it be? Consider the benefits now and in the future, and consider the expectations you may or may not have set in your life as it pertains to this question. If you choose to answer the question, you must commit to work diligently to accomplish it. You owe it to yourself.

There are so many Christians today who give Jesus Christ five minutes of their hectic day while devoting countless hours per day to television and movies. Others find themselves committed to their careers ten to twelve hours per day while giving an average of eight minutes per day to their children.

The wisest, most successful man to ever walk the earth once said this about life: "I denied myself nothing my eyes desired; I refused my heart no pleasure. My heart took delight in all my work, and this was the reward for all my labor. Yet when I surveyed all that my hands had done and what I had toiled to achieve, everything was meaningless, a chasing after the wind; nothing was gained under the sun."[4] Today, confirm that your effort truly matches your priorities.

As you begin to step up in the important areas of your life, you will take great pride and satisfaction in knowing that you are becoming intentional and living with purpose. If you commit to developing a strong work ethic in the most important areas of your life, you will change the very course of your life and begin to experience a completely new level of quality in your life. Red McCombs once said, "We all have twenty-four hours a day. What will you do with your twenty-four hours?"

CHAPTER 10

Leadership

"Everything rises and falls on leadership."

JOHN MAXWELL

"The challenge of leadership is to be strong, but not rude; be kind, but not weak; be bold, but not bully; be thoughtful, but not lazy; be humble, but not timid; be proud, but not arrogant; have humor, but without folly."

JIM ROHN

Leadership is not a position. It is not a title or a level of authority, and it is often misunderstood and improperly applied. Leadership is not shaped in a cookie-cutter process. Leadership should not be confused with management. Leaders are not born. Leaders are not superhuman. Leaders are not perfect. Leaders should not be copied, cloned, or counterfeited.

You were called to be a leader!

You may disagree, but you have been called to leadership whether you like it or not. Every person in the world has some sphere of influence, and you have yours. You may feel unqualified and incompetent to lead, but you do have influence on those around you, so you must decide what you will do about it.

There is good news. You have the potential and the opportunity to be a life-changing leader regardless of your background, personal traits, lack of experience, past mistakes, or limited abilities. In fact, only you can step into the unique leadership role God has for you. There is no one else in the world who can fill your role. Leadership is like a fingerprint. It should be unique and specific to you.

In this chapter, you are going to learn several key principles to effective leadership, but you must take these principles and apply them to your unique style and personality.

I have discovered that the great entrepreneurs have utilized core leadership principles, and they have applied those principles in extremely unique ways. Authentic leadership requires you to develop your leadership style as an original. It will not be possible to copy another person's leadership style and achieve authentic leadership. In the pages that follow, you are going to learn some extraordinary principles to leadership, but your application of those principles must be within your unique style.

There is much at stake, and you have the potential to influence others to do great things. John Maxwell makes a bold statement in his book *Developing the Leader within You*: "Everything rises and falls on leadership."[1] The importance of effective leadership cannot be measured, because people's lives are in the balance. Everything does in fact rise and fall on leadership. The Bible says, "Without wise leadership, a nation falls."[2]

In your life right now, there are people who are looking to you for leadership. It may not be in a formal sense, but you do have some measure of influence. You also have the ability to learn leadership principles and put them into practice in your own unique way.

If you are questioning whether you have what it takes to be the leader God has called you to be, you're in good company! Moses also thought he did not have what it would take to be the leader God was calling him to be.

God came to Moses one day, spoke to him through a burning bush, and called him to approach Pharaoh in Egypt in order to lead the Israelites out of captivity. It's not like Moses had been attending leadership courses and was on the verge of graduating with an official certificate in effective leadership. In fact, Moses's resume at this point was nonexistent. What was Moses doing at the moment God called him? He was taking care of some sheep for his father-in-law. That's not exactly the experience you would expect to lead to the role of guiding the entire Israelite population out of slavery.

I can identify with Moses's response to God after he was asked to approach Pharaoh. Moses said, "Who am I, that I should go to Pharaoh and bring the Israelites out of Egypt?"[3] Moses continued to explain to God why he was not able to lead: "Pardon your servant, Lord. I have never been eloquent, neither in the past nor since you have spoken to your servant. I am slow of speech and tongue." Moses went so far as to recommend someone else. He told God, "Pardon your servant, Lord. Please send someone else."[4]

I want to encourage you today that you have exactly what it takes to lead. God created you precisely as you are. You do not have to become someone else in order to lead. You need to become you. The leadership principles outlined in this chapter are tools that you can use and apply, but I assure you that you already have everything that you need to lead. God provided a response to Moses's litany of reasons why he was not able to lead. God's response was, "I will be with you."[5]

As you begin to learn and apply the following principles on leadership, remember that your leadership style should be unique to you as God designed you to be.

DEFINING LEADERSHIP

Let's begin by defining leadership, because the misconceptions about leadership are enormous. John Maxwell defines leadership as, "Leadership is influence. That's it. Nothing more; nothing less."[6] Influence will typically be the natural effect of a leader's lifestyle and behavior on others. Please note that Maxwell's definition of leadership does not differentiate good leadership from bad. A person can have great influence over others, or that influence can be negative. We will obviously be referring to the positive attributes of leadership in this chapter, but you should never forget that you *do* have the power to influence others—for good or for bad.

I also want to make it clear that leadership is much more than simply leading people. If leadership is influence, then it also includes your influence over yourself. In many ways, leadership begins with leading yourself. If you cannot find influence over yourself, then you will struggle to find influence over others.

Lesson 1: LEADERSHIP SOMETIMES HURTS

Imagine for a moment that you have joined the United States Marine Corps. My uncle Larry enlisted in the Marines in the late 1950s, and he was one of many Marines on standby during the Cuban Missile Crisis. In late October of 1962, President Kennedy declared DEFCON 2, and my uncle found himself aboard one of the many ships in a naval quarantine of Cuba.

During that alarming, tumultuous time, my uncle patiently waited. He would be one of the first Marines on the ground if an invasion was ordered. Although he was concerned and nervous, he had also been prepared for the situation. He knew there would be an enemy he would be fighting. He was fully aware of the risks involved.

Can you imagine training to be a Marine and never being told you would face fire from the enemy? What a shock it would be the first time you were sent to fight in a foreign war, and suddenly you realized there were men on the other side with guns who wanted to kill you!

Can you imagine the fear and surprise you would feel in that situation? You might second-guess the decision you made to join, and maybe you would feel a bit deceived. You certainly would not be equipped to fight if you were never trained to handle battle situations.

The same is true for those who find themselves in a leadership position without any knowledge of the following facts. Below are just a few of the realities that come with leadership:

Reality 1: As a Leader, You Will Be Second-Guessed. I guarantee that at some point, if you are in a leadership role, you are going to be shot at. Maybe not with real bullets, but there will be those who will work to undermine your efforts. There will be people, possibly good friends, who will criticize you, attack you, talk about you behind your back, and disagree with every direction you attempt to take. You will be second-guessed, and you will find it is impossible to please everyone you are leading.

Several years ago, an old coworker and friend of mine was promoted to a significant leadership role within the company I was working for at the time. Prior to his promotion, he couldn't wait to be in a position of leadership. He had an ability to see the mistakes of our previous leader, and he knew exactly how he would handle each situation. Unfortunately, the company was a smaller organization without a formal leadership and training process. When employees received a promotion and were placed in command for the first time in their lives, they received "on the job" training, which meant they didn't receive any training at all.

My friend only lasted about two months in his new role before he couldn't take it any longer. He soon took a new job with a different company. He later shared with me his shock and disappointment with his short stint as a manager. My friend was amazed at how different his experience was from his original expectations. Several of his subordinates did not agree with his initiatives and plans for the team. There were constant grumblings, and he was not equipped to deal with the situation. There were people he thought he could trust who clearly undermined his position, and he had a difficult time just surviving. He swore he would never seek out a leadership position again.

Reality 2: Some People Will Want to See You Fail No Matter What. Unfortunately this is true, and it is important to recognize it in advance, because you may end up leading someone who will never be happy with you. You have to be willing to accept this truth and move on. You will discover as a leader that you cannot make people like you. If you are unwilling to accept this truth, you are heading for a lot of heartache. While this situation is not necessarily common, it has the potential to be reality.

Reality 3: You Can't Please Everyone. With virtually every decision you make, there will be people who will be happy, people who will be angry, and people who will not care either way. Your understanding of this truth will give you the confidence to make the best decision that you can regardless of what people think.

Reality 4: Leadership Can Sometimes Be a Lonely Role. Just remember that at times as a leader, you will feel alone. It is normal, and you may experience this feeling from time to time. I hope I haven't scared you too much! I have found that when you have realistic expectations, the difficult aspects of leadership are much easier to deal with.

LESSON 2: YOU NEED A LEADERSHIP POWER SOURCE.

In order to be an effective leader, you will need to draw your leadership power from a source, just as an electronic device requires a power source. An electronic device may use AC power or a battery pack to draw the necessary power to operate. In much the same way, you will need a power source to fuel you as a leader. Many leaders will find that power source within themselves. They will rely on their own thoughts and plans as they lead. Others may use people close to them for support. I would like to make a case for using God as your leadership power source.

I referenced Moses as an example at the beginning of this chapter, because Moses is an amazing example of a leader who grounded himself in a foundation based on God. Moses transformed from a frightened shepherd with little self-confidence into an incredible leader. He confronted Pharaoh with conviction. He rallied the Israelites and led them through the parting of the Red Sea out of slavery and into freedom. Moses delivered the Ten Commandments from God to the people, and he effectively managed the nation of Israel through a difficult forty years in the desert.

Moses accomplished these amazing things because he relied on God to fulfill his promise. Remember that God told Moses, "I will be with you." God will also be with you, but the decision to plug into him or not is yours. He will not force himself upon you, so you are free to decide if you will rely on God's power or your own.

Your relationship to God will provide you with a level of confidence that will be significant to your leadership abilities. You may be thinking to yourself right now, "I will never be fully prepared to be the leader God wants me to be." The real truth is that if you ask God for wisdom, he will give it to you. The Bible says, "If any of you lacks wisdom, he should ask God, who gives generously to all without finding fault, and it will be given to him."[7]

King Solomon is considered to be the wisest man to walk the earth. When he first became king of Israel, he was given the opportunity to ask for anything his heart desired. Can you imagine having the opportunity to ask for anything that you want? Here was Solomon's response: "Give me wisdom and knowledge, that I may lead this people, for who is able to govern this great people of yours?"[8] I think it is amazing that Solomon asked for wisdom and leadership from God. And guess what? God gave it to him.

God provides confidence and wisdom, and these attributes are a powerhouse combination for effective leadership. The Bible says, "Though an army may encamp against me, my heart shall not fear; though war may rise against me, in this I will be confident."[9] There will be moments as a leader when you are going to face difficulty, and those people you are leading will look to you for leadership. Your confidence will be the soothing and reassuring encouragement they need to make it through.

The Bible says, "For the Spirit God gave us does not make us timid, but gives us power, love, and self-discipline."[10] If you are timid, second-guessing yourself, and worried, then you'd better check your power source. The closer you get to God, the greater your confidence will be, and that confidence will translate into powerful leadership.

LESSON 3: RESPONSIBILITY IS ESSENTIAL

Winston Churchill once said, "The price of greatness is responsibility." When you dissect the meaning of *responsibility,* you essentially arrive at this definition: the ability to respond. If you are going to lead others to a particular destination and expect them to follow, then you must be willing to go to that destination yourself. Self-discipline is extremely important in effective leadership.

As a leader you are responsible for those whom you lead, but you are also responsible for yourself and your own actions. Be sure that you are setting the best example possible.

Lesson 4: Always Do What Is Right, and When Placed in Command, Take Charge

I had the great opportunity to see General Normal Schwarzkopf speak several years ago at a leadership conference, and he made a statement that impacted me in a dramatic way. He said, "Always do what is right, and when placed in command, take charge."

Those two principles are essential to effective leadership. I made the mistake early on in my leadership journey of letting the caboose drive the train because I didn't have enough confidence in my own judgment. Inexperienced leaders will sometimes acquiesce to those whom they lead, and as a result, they allow the opinions of their followers to drive their decision-making. Take note of this important lesson: when placed in command, take charge.

This is how you learn to be a leader. You will make mistakes, and your judgment will never be perfect. It's all right to make mistakes—all leaders do—but you cannot lead if you elevate the opinions of your team above your own. There is great wisdom in seeking the thoughts and opinions of your team, but you are the one to call that final shot. Do not let anyone else make that decision for you.

Take in all the advice and opinions and then draw your own conclusions. If the people you are leading sense for a second that you are indecisive and waffling on an issue, they will not respect you. In your effort to appease them, you'll lose them.

People want to follow a leader who is not afraid to lead, and they will rarely follow a leader who hesitates. It's perfectly acceptable to seek advice and counsel prior to making a decision, but the one who is leading is responsible for stepping up to the plate and making the decision.

Do not apologize for your decisions, especially if you choose against someone's advice. Advice is only advice, but the leader has to gather all the data together in order to make the best decision. This is the job of a leader, so don't be afraid to do it.

I sometimes struggled with leading individuals who were more qualified and more experienced than me. I would sometimes wonder if they were second-guessing my leadership and direction. It was not until I learned this valuable leadership principle that I later realized that you will always be second-guessed. It comes with the territory. Instead of worrying about what other people thought was or wasn't the right decision, I started leading. I soon discovered that you don't have to be the smartest person in the room to lead. I'm an excellent example of that truth!

I do want to emphasize how important it is to solicit feedback and advice from key team members who can impart critical information to assist in the decision-making process. It is extremely important and valuable to have a team that can express opinions openly and honestly without judgment. The Bible says, "Plans fail for lack of counsel, but with many advisers they succeed."[11] Your team should always feel safe to disagree with you and express their thoughts. But in the end, the leader calls the final shot. You cannot be successful any other way.

I participated in an organization for a while under the leadership of a man who struggled to take charge. He was an incredible person, with great integrity and excellent ideas, but he struggled to take a stand or head in a particular direction if he thought he didn't have 100 percent agreement.

He always crafted his statements with great care so as to not offend anyone who might disagree with him. I recall a meeting one time that required some critical decision-making. The leader waited for quite some time as members of the team voiced their opinions until he sensed where the majority stood. Once that was clear, he stood before the team and made this statement: "I always lead by waiting to see what the consensus is first, and then I know what direction we should take." It's interesting, because he later shared with me that the decision he made was not a decision he really agreed with.

I will tell you that leading in this way is not leading at all. It's called following. What if the consensus was heading in a direction that you knew was certain failure? What if the consensus was heading down a path that was immoral? How can you be leading when you are waiting for a consensus? The only time as a leader that you should be waiting for direction is when you are waiting on God.

There are many politicians today who lead by waiting to see what the polls are saying. Leadership by consensus is anything but leadership. Unfortunately, this leader struggled in setting the course for this organization, because he was unwilling to truly lead. I still have great respect and admiration for him, but his lack of leadership crippled his ability to guide the organization forward to reach its full potential. Francis Frangipane once said, "To inoculate me from the praise of man, He baptized me in the criticism of man, until I died to the control of man."[12]

After you have taken charge as a leader, then do what is right. Take note of General Schwarzkopf's statement: do what is right. He didn't say to do what other people think is right or to do what is popular, he said, "Do what is right."

I have discovered in my own life that there are millions of ways to bend the truth, push the limits, and justify gray areas, and it is much easier to achieve so-called success by taking shortcuts and cheating. Doing what is right, on the other hand, is usually the harder path to take, at least in the beginning.

Many professional athletes have discovered that using steroids can catapult their athletic ability faster and more effectively than working hard in the gym the old-fashioned way. Countless politicians have learned that taking bribes and backdoor agreements can get you ahead much faster than being honest and legal. Chuck Colson once said, "I learned one thing in Watergate: I was well-intentioned but rationalized illegal behavior… You cannot live your life other than walking in the truth. Your means are as important as your ends."

We all discover that in everyday life, we are faced with decisions that either take us down the high road or the low road. This issue multiplies when we step into a leadership role, and the consequences multiply exponentially.

Doing what is right will protect you every single time in the long run, and it will protect those whom you lead. The Bible says, "There is nothing concealed that will not be disclosed, or hidden that will not be made known."[13] I assure you that if you choose to take the shortcut, your actions will be revealed someday, and you will pay tenfold. The easy road in the beginning leads to disaster in the end.

Most people who find themselves in a major scandal arrived there through small compromises. Small compromises are deadly killers that appear harmless in the beginning. My family loves boating and water sports, and we spend a great deal of time on the water during the summer months. One activity that our children absolutely enjoy is swimming in the lake. We usually park our boat at the end of a favorite cove after several hours of wakeboarding and skiing, and we all spend some time splashing and swimming while the boat just floats along nearby.

On one occasion, we all became preoccupied with the idea of splashing and swimming so much that we soon lost track of our boat. In a very short period of time, the boat had floated several hundred yards away from us and was heading for the shore. We had to swim frantically to catch it in time, and I was amazed at how far it went without any of us noticing.

Our lives are very similar. We never set out to commit great offenses in the beginning, but we start with very small compromises. The man who finds himself in adultery usually doesn't start his marriage off with that goal in mind. But as he chooses to make small compromises over time, he finds himself very far from his initial intentions.

The small compromises are the deadliest decisions we can make, because we don't see the consequences immediately. Consequences do not usually become evident until it's too late and we are already well down the path of destruction.

Our moral decisions not only affect our lives, but the lives of those around us. The decisions you make today will have a lasting impact on your life and on almost everyone who comes into contact with you. Most people tend to compartmentalize their lives, especially when making compromises. We never think that the decisions we make in the work environment might one day affect the decisions our children make.

Always do what is right, and you never have to fear. If your actions come into question, you will have no skeletons in your closet keeping you up late at night. Your reputation and honor will be recognized, and you will never regret choices you've made in the past.

It sounds so easy, doesn't it? But it can be very difficult to do. It is often the right choices that are the difficult choices. Become addicted to making right choices. Make it a lifestyle and a habit.

Maybe you are reading this now, and you are feeling convicted and disappointed. Maybe you're already down that low road, and you feel like you're in too deep. Make this your day of reckoning. Actively choose to make things right by admitting your mistakes and take the appropriate corrective action. There is great honor in owning up to your mistakes and being transparent, especially if you do so before you're forced to do so.

The Bible references a tax collector, Zacchaeus, who was confronted head on with the Savior of the world, Jesus Christ. Zacchaeus was a tax collector in Jericho, and it is very probable that he had been cheating honest taxpayers for years. Most tax collectors of that day were guilty of taking far beyond the government's fair share for their own personal gain.

Zacchaeus was touched by Jesus's message, and he soon realized the path he'd been heading down. Zacchaeus took immediate action. He said to Jesus, "Look, Lord! Here and now I give half of my possessions to the poor, and if I have cheated anybody out of anything, I will pay back four times the amount."[14] Jesus then commended Zacchaeus for his decision. Zacchaeus could have crawled away in shame and guilt, but instead he made things right.

These two components of leadership will provide a powerful framework for your leadership approach. When placed in command, take charge, and always do what is right. I guarantee if you apply this leadership lesson in your life, you will be well on your way to becoming an effective leader.

LESSON 5: TRUST AND TRANSPARENCY

Can you think of anyone you would be willing to follow whom you don't trust? Would you be willing to follow someone who has issues with honesty? Could you follow someone who would be willing to sacrifice you in an effort to protect himself? The answers to these questions are obvious, and you should note their significance when you consider the kind of leader you are striving to be.

Trust is absolutely critical to leading effectively. The people you lead need to know that you will do what you say, and they need to know that they can count on your word. They also need to know that you will support them and back them up as their leader. If these attributes are not apparent in you, you will never lead effectively.

Moses certainly had the trust of the Israelite people when he led them out of Egypt and across the Red Sea while the Egyptians chased after them. Any Israelite following Moses at that time had grown up in Egypt as a slave, and slavery is the only life they had ever known. Can you imagine the Israelites following Moses if he'd been known to stretch the truth from time to time? What if Moses had a reputation of only taking care of himself? Would anyone be willing to risk their lives and the lives of their families by placing their trust in Moses if he had such a reputation? Our character and word have great significance in our effectiveness as leaders.

I have worked for several people over the years, but two bosses stand out to me as great examples of what to do and what not to do as it relates to trust in a leader. My very first boss in my first job out of college was an incredible example of a leader who established trust, rapport, and confidence with consistency. Jeanne invested great time, effort, and risk in me as a new employee. She did a very good job of training me in my position, but more than that, she had an unbelievable talent for uncovering my strengths and potential.

She went out of her way to create opportunities for me to shine in my role, and these opportunities also came with risk. In one such opportunity, I made a mistake, and the mistake became visible to Jeanne's boss and her boss's boss.

The entire situation came to a head in a meeting with several key decision makers, including Jeanne. It would have been very easy for Jeanne to simply place the blame on me. I was, after all, the source of the problem in this particular situation. Although I hadn't done anything intentional and the mistake was simply a result of my lack of experience, Jeanne could have easily saved herself a lot of trouble by pointing the blame in my direction. But she chose a different route. She protected me and backed me up, and I know she spent some political capital with her bosses in the process. She stood behind me, and she defended me by defending my ability to take risks and make mistakes. We do tend to learn the most from our mistakes.

Several months later, as a result of Jeanne's actions and constant support, I was placed into a fast-track role in the organization. During my interview panels, I was able to reference this specific incident as an incredible turnaround opportunity and learning experience.

What could have been a deathblow to my early career ended up being a great turning point, and it was an excellent learning experience for me. Why? I had a leader in my life who was looking out for my best interests. Jeanne earned my trust and respect. I would have sacrificed my job in a heartbeat for her, because I knew she would do the same for me. I knew I could trust her, because she demonstrated that fact on a regular basis. I will tell you that this trait is not very prevalent in corporate America today.

I also realized that Jeanne's entire team felt exactly as I did. One of my coworkers put it this way: "I've been with this company for twenty-five years, and I've never worked for someone who believes in me like Jeanne does." I found myself working my heart out in that position. The key motivating factor behind my hard work was my desire not to let Jeanne down. I didn't want to disappoint her. I trusted her and respected her a great deal.

If you want to effectively lead people and create opportunities for them to grow and develop beyond where they are today, you have to build genuine trust.

Several years later, I had the opportunity to work for a boss who was the exact opposite of Jeanne. It was very difficult working for someone I didn't trust or respect. It was also difficult getting motivated to do my best. I witnessed my boss in situations where he betrayed trust, cheated, and lied, and he always did what was in his best interest.

Although this individual was my boss and I reported directly to him, he was not my leader. I looked to other individuals in the organization for leadership, and I just did my best to survive the situation. As I look back on it now, it was a great learning experience for me. I had the opportunity to see what happens when you don't have the trust of those you are leading. I also witnessed the devastating results of broken trust and deception. (My boss eventually left the company.)

Building trust and rapport can be challenging at times, because we are all human beings with a sinful nature. That means you will make mistakes, and most of your mistakes and shortcomings will be on display when you're in a leadership role.

But I have a great solution that will overcome your flawed nature and future mistakes as you strive to be a great leader. It is called transparency. Whenever you make a mistake as a leader, take immediate responsibility and correct the situation as fast as you possibly can. After the problem is corrected, admit your mistakes and apologize as appropriate. Never deviate from this pattern.

If you try to cover or hide your mistakes or simply refuse to admit to them, you will destroy credibility and trust with those around you. However, the opposite is true when you own up to your shortcomings and mistakes. By demonstrating transparency and responsibility, you don't just correct the immediate issue in front of you, but you actually increase the level of trust and respect of those around you.

I am always impressed with great leaders who take responsibility for their actions. I find myself admiring those who have the guts to own up to their mistakes and share what they've learned from them. These situations also keep us humble, and God always honors those who are humble. The Bible says, "He guides the humble in what is right and teaches them his way."[15] It also says, "For those who exalt themselves will be humbled, and those who humble themselves will be exalted."[16]

My dad always demonstrated this trait as I was growing up. Whenever he made a mistake, he came to me, looked me in the eye, and quickly apologized and owned up to the mistake. My respect and admiration for him always increased when he did this.

Consider great leaders from the past who have successfully exercised this trait. When Dwight D. Eisenhower ordered the D-Day invasion on the sixth of June in 1944, he composed a letter that would go out in case of defeat. The importance of this invasion was astronomical. The fate of the world was essentially hanging on the success of this incredible invasion of Normandy. The invasion would kick off the Western Allied effort to liberate mainland Europe from Nazi occupation. It was the largest invasion force in human history, with over seven thousand ships operated by 195,000 naval personnel from eight allied countries and approximately 130,000 troops. Do you think Eisenhower was dealing with some pressure? His decisions would affect millions of lives and the entire world at that time.

The final decision for D-Day rested on Eisenhower's shoulders. Although there were countless individuals involved in the process, he was the final decision maker. He was the one to call the final shot for proceeding. The invasion had already been pushed by a month to June 5, and the weather forced Eisenhower to settle with June 6 as the final date. Meteorologists predicted a break in the weather, and Eisenhower called the shot.

Here's what he wrote in the letter he prepared if the invasion failed:

Our landings in the Cherbourg-Harve area have failed to gain a satisfactory foothold and I have withdrawn the troops. My decision to attack at this time and place was based upon the best information available. The troops, the air and the Navy did all that bravery and devotion to duty could do. If any blame or fault attaches to the attempt it is mine alone.[17]

Although this letter was not necessary because of the success of the Allied forces, Eisenhower was prepared to take full responsibility no matter what the outcome.

I can also point to countless examples of failed leadership as it relates to responsibility. President Bill Clinton repeatedly denied involvement in a relationship with Monica Lewinsky, a White House intern, and he did so publicly on television and privately to those closest to him. Only when his back was against the wall and it was inevitable that the truth would become public did he recant and openly admit his mistakes. To add injury to insult, he also had to admit that he was lying and covering up his affair. His actions led to an impeachment and a loss of trust and respect for the president of the United States.[18]

Another president made similar mistakes in an even worse situation when he consistently covered up his illegal actions and involvement in a scandal called Watergate. President Richard Nixon left the White House in shame and dishonor, becoming the first US president in history to resign his position.[19]

John F. Kennedy, on the other hand, demonstrated leadership transparency after the failed American invasion of Cuba, known as the Bay of Pigs, in 1961. The entire situation was very embarrassing for the United States, and President Kennedy had to respond following the failed attempt. Although Kennedy made several changes in the CIA following this fiasco, he did take public responsibility for the entire situation. "There's an old saying that victory has a hundred fathers and defeat is an orphan," Kennedy said, adding, "I am the responsible officer of the government."

Once President Kennedy accepted responsibility for the disaster, he took immediate action to change up the national security team and process that had failed him. Kennedy put in place an executive committee including both current and former cabinet members (including Republicans) to ensure multiple perspectives in times of crisis.

Just one year later, Kennedy's new approach and experience were a key component to the successful resolution of the Cuban Missile Crisis. Kennedy admitted his mistakes, learned from them, and was transparent about the process.[20] As a result, we admire Kennedy for those actions.

It is imperative that you establish trust, honesty, and transparency in order to be an effective leader.

LESSON 6: DEMONSTRATE LOVE THROUGH ACTION

A leader must genuinely love those he or she leads, and love is only truly demonstrated through action. You can say "I love you," but your words are meaningless if your actions contradict them. Andrew Carnegie once said, "As I grow older, I pay less attention to what men say. I just watch what they do."

General Schwarzkopf demonstrated his love for the men under his command in an incident in Vietnam, and those men never forgot it. In March of 1970, Schwarzkopf was informed that some of the men in his command had become trapped in a minefield. He immediately rushed to that location in his helicopter, and he ordered his men to retrace their steps. Unfortunately they were struggling to identify the mines, and his men were dying with every wrong step. It would have been very easy for Schwarzkopf to direct his men via radio from the safety of his helicopter, but instead, he did something that shocked everyone.

Schwarzkopf got out of his helicopter, and he got into the minefield. One of his men had tripped a mine, and he was injured and still conscious. Schwarzkopf held him down so another soldier could splint his leg. Schwarzkopf eventually led his men out of the minefield despite being injured himself by one of the explosions. He demonstrated to everyone that he was willing to risk his life for the soldiers under his command. He could have given a million speeches on his love for the troops, but his actions told the entire story.[21]

A leader who demonstrates love through action solidifies unparalleled allegiance and respect. My dad consistently demonstrated his love for the employees under his command as president of the Terminal Railroad, and those employees expressed their gratitude back in their own actions during a very difficult situation in his career. Hurricane Katrina struck Louisiana on August 29, 2005, and caused severe destruction across the southern part of the United States. The effects of that disaster rippled across the United States, paralyzing the rail network. As a result, the Terminal Railroad, a major rail hub and switching operation in the Metro St. Louis area, came to a screeching halt.

My dad found himself working with all the major railroads across the United States in an effort to move and navigate rail traffic. He was working eighteen-hour days, and his job as president was in jeopardy. Over the years prior to this event, my dad had built a reputation for protecting his employees and placing their needs above his own. In an unprecedented event, his employees worked additional days and hours for no pay in order to help. His team rallied behind him, and he was later awarded the "Man of the Year" rail award for his efforts and leadership during the Katrina crisis.

Perhaps the greatest example in all of history of love demonstrated through action is that of Jesus Christ. Jesus came and willingly chose to hang and die on a cross for all of mankind. He was perfectly innocent, and yet he took the bullet on my behalf and yours. He absolutely demonstrated love. I find it fascinating what happened after Jesus rose again from the tomb and then ascended into heaven. It has been reported that his disciples all went on to die martyrs' deaths. It has also been reported that Peter even died as a martyr on a cross—upside down, at his own request. He made the request because he felt he was not worthy to be crucified as Christ was.[22]

There are two things that explain why these disciples all chose to share the gospel and eventually die as martyrs. First, they knew without a doubt that Jesus Christ really was God when they witnessed his resurrection. There is no other explanation for their behavior. If they had not witnessed the resurrection, it is hard to believe they all would have chosen to die, knowing they would be dying for a lie. Second, they knew how much Jesus loved them. Jesus's love for them was the motivation to live and die as martyrs. His love was clearly demonstrated on the cross.

As a leader, you need to demonstrate your love for those whom you have the responsibility of leading. The benefits can never be measured.

LESSON 7: BE DECISIVE

We all make decisions every day, and every decision has consequences that have some degree of impact on our lives. Several years ago, I struggled with making tough decisions, especially when I was faced with multiple choices that all seemed good. I always wanted to keep my options open, and a decision inherently blocks all options but the one you choose. To decide means to cut yourself off from any other choice.

It was painful for me to be cutting off choices that were good choices. What if the choice I made appeared to be good, but ended in disaster? What if I could have made a better choice? As a result, I hesitated to make tough decisions by not making any decision at all. This strategy is a common one among those who fear decision-making.

I learned over time that by not making a decision, I was actually making a decision. In every case, I unintentionally made a bad decision through indecision. For example, when I was a freshman in college, I considered trying out for the soccer team as a walk-on after recovering from a broken leg in high school. I had been playing on a league team at the time, and I thought that maybe I could try out and possibly make the B team at my college. It would be a great experience, and I would get plenty of exercise and the enjoyment of playing. I talked with the coach at my college and he invited me to try out. I also weighed out the time commitment and my other activities I was involved in. I was really torn, and I just couldn't decide what to do.

Eventually my freshman year ended, and I considered trying out my sophomore year. Before I knew it, I was a senior. I never made it to tryouts. You could say that I never made a decision, but I certainly did. I decided not to try out by not making a decision to try out. As I look back at it now, I should have gone to tryouts. I really wanted to, but I made my choice by not making one. My indecision led to decision, and it was a decision I regret making.

In the book *Think and Grow Rich*, Napoleon Hill stated, "Analysis of over 25,000 men and women who had experienced failure disclosed the fact that lack of decision was near the head of the list of the thirty-one major causes of failure."[23]

Another component of indecision is the paralyzing thing called procrastination. I have struggled in the past with this leadership killer, and it is a debilitating disease that you must conquer in order to be an effective leader. I urge you to procrastinate on your procrastination by taking urgent and immediate action.

My leadership abilities changed profoundly after I realized the effect that indecision had on my life. Napoleon Hill wrote this about Henry Ford: "One of Henry Ford's most outstanding qualities was his habit of reaching decisions quickly and definitely, and changing them slowly."[24]

Hill also wrote, "Analysis of several hundred people who had accumulated fortunes well beyond the million-dollar mark disclosed the fact that every one of them had the habit of reaching decisions promptly, and of changing these decisions slowly, if, and when they were changed."[25]

I have found that people who struggle to lead effectively struggle to make decisions in a timely manner, and they tend to change their decisions regularly. As a person who always worked to keep his options open, I found myself vacillating from one idea to the next without ever really taking a stand by making a decision on the most important ideas.

It is imperative that you learn to make effective decisions as quickly as you can, and you must hold the line on those decisions through thick and thin. I believe it wise to always leave room for a change, but that change should be made slowly and with great care. Bouncing back and forth from one decision to the next will not only render you useless, but it will also destroy any confidence your followers might have in your leadership abilities.

I realize this is a terrifying proposition, because making decisions is a risky business. Whenever we make a decision, we also take responsibility for the outcome of that decision. People who live in fear fail to be decisive because they are afraid of the risk. I can't tell you what an incredible relief it is to live life without fear and without indecision! I know—because this very principle changed my entire life.

Several years ago, I made a conscious choice to become decisive. I started with small decisions, quickly weighing out the options and then choosing the best option based on the information I had at the time. I focused on committing to that decision with resolve and determination.

Once you've committed to a decision, you no longer waste your time in turmoil and indecision. You are now free to focus on the next steps and moving forward. If you are faced with a decision that involves two equally good choices and you cannot rank one over the other, then flip a coin and commit to one.

You can't ride two different horses across the finish line at the same time.

I do want to point out that becoming decisive does not mean making decisions in a cavalier fashion with no regard to weighing out the options and possible consequences. It simply means that once you've done your homework, you make a decision and then live by it.

Sometimes it will take time to gather information and seek advice from trusted advisers in addition to seeking God's wisdom and will for a particular decision. Once that direction is clear, then you must do the difficult part: decide and move forward. Being decisive will set you on a course to great leadership.

LESSON 8: ADDRESS POTENTIAL PROBLEMS DIRECTLY AND AGGRESSIVELY

One consistent area of trouble for leaders is the avoidance of conflict and potential problems. People will sometimes do anything to avoid a confrontation or potential problem, including simply ignoring the issue and hoping that it goes away on its own. In most cases, a potential problem that is ignored will eventually grow into a much larger problem.

My mom experienced this several years ago with her car. The check engine light on the dashboard of her car came on, and she ignored it. She continued to ignore the warning, hoping that it would eventually go away. I think that over a period of several days she grew accustomed to seeing the light on. She may have even questioned the validity of the warning since the car continued to start and run day after day.

Eventually the day of reckoning came when her car experienced a catastrophic failure. I'll never forget my dad asking my mom why she didn't tell him about the check engine light. The actual cause of the engine failure was due to a lack of oil. For less than a dollar or two and five minutes of time, oil could have been added to the motor. Countless hours and thousands of dollars could have been saved. The same is often true in our own lives when we ignore warning lights in our personal lives—not to mention emotional, mental, and spiritual costs.

You know the warning lights I am referencing. You sense a strained relationship with someone close, but you're too afraid to address it. Your health starts to turn because you are not eating right and exercising. You find yourself saying and doing things you would have never done in the past because your spiritual walk with God is slipping. Your spouse seems distant and distracted, but you don't stop to ask why.

As a leader, you will have similar warning lights. If you have a habit of ignoring those warning lights, then you could be heading into a storm. It takes awareness, discipline, and courage to address potential problems directly and aggressively. I assure you that a proactive approach will eliminate 80 percent of the problems you will face as a leader.

I learned this lesson a few years ago on a real-estate project I was involved in. I had contracted with a construction company to build a spec house, and I started to see some warning lights from the contractor from the very beginning. This contractor had a habit of dishonesty and telling me what I wanted to hear instead of what I needed to hear. I sensed it from the beginning, but I wanted to avoid any confrontation. As the project continued on, mistakes were made, and I caught the contractor changing his story.

At this point in the project, I should have addressed him directly with my concerns. I could have threatened to end the project immediately, and I could have started getting things in writing. Unfortunately, I did not take these proactive measures. Instead, I just hoped the problems would go away and everything would end happily ever after. I'm sure you can guess that this was not how it ended.

Instead, I had quite a mess on my hands at the end. Most of the disaster could have been avoided if I had tackled those issues head-on. Taking on potential problems before they start is like taking medicine. It might not taste very good, but it will save you from bigger problems down the road.

LESSON 9: KEEP A COOL HEAD

As a leader, you will face problems. Whenever you do, you need to keep a cool head. I refer to this as the Bruce Willis effect. In almost every Bruce Willis film that I've ever seen, Willis's character always stays calm, cool, and collected. It's important when you are facing a crisis to keep a cool head and stay calm. If you are out of control mentally and emotionally, how will you be able to use your head to navigate the stormy waters?

Not only that, but if you are visibly out of control, how do you think the people you are leading will be affected? Can you imagine being a passenger in an airplane with a pilot who's weeping uncontrollably as the plane hits turbulence? How much confidence would you have in the pilot at that point?

I'll never forget hearing a story from the founder and CEO of Curves International, a fitness franchise company. I used to own several Curves locations, and I had a chance to hear Gary Heavin speak at Curves headquarters in Texas several years ago. Zig Ziglar was also there that day with Gary, and Gary shared a story that impacted me a great deal.

Gary holds a private pilot's license, and he flies his personal plane all over the world in his spare time. Gary shared his experience of crash-landing into a swamp one night. He recalled the experience with great intensity and detail. The engine failed, and oil from the engine started spewing all over the front window of the plane. He knew he was going down, and he couldn't see anything in front of him.

I think that at this point in the story, most people would be completely out of control. Gary was tempted to give up and emotionally check out. The odds were stacked against him, and he was terrified. But then he remembered Zig Ziglar's outstanding advice on how to deal with a crisis.

I recall hearing Zig speak several years ago about this very topic. Zig shared that you *respond* to a crisis, you don't *react* to one. You must keep an even keel and stay focused on the task at hand without losing control. Zig referenced President Ronald Reagan's response after he was shot in an assassination attempt on March 30, 1981. Shortly after the shooting, President Reagan was rushed to

George Washington University Hospital. Upon arriving, he got out and walked unassisted to the emergency room with a bullet lodged in his lung that had just missed his heart. Reagan joked with the operating doctor just before surgery by saying, "Doctor, I hope you are Republican." When his wife Nancy arrived at the hospital, he told her, "Honey, I forgot to duck."

President Reagan kept a cool head and stayed calm despite the circumstances. He demonstrated incredible leadership to those around him and to the nation when his very life was in jeopardy.[26]

Gary Heavin applied Zig's advice as his plane was headed for imminent disaster. He immediately collected himself and focused on the task at hand. He did everything he could do to bring the plane down as smoothly as possible, and he ended up crash-landing into a swamp. Gary survived the crash, and he credited Zig Ziglar with saving his life. Gary shared that if he had not stayed calm throughout the situation, he never would have survived.

Thomas Jefferson once said, "Nothing gives a person so much advantage over another as to remain always cool and unruffled under all circumstances."

Lesson 10: Inspire Others to Be Part of Something Great

Most people aspire to be part of something big, but it is rare that they ever participate in an environment of great things. The majority of people in the workforce today do their jobs because they have to and not because they want to. If you have ever been part of a group or organization that has achieved an aura of belonging and teamwork with inspiration and excitement, then you know how incredible it can be to be an active participant in that environment. You find yourself with enormous motivation, and you look forward to contributing in any way that you can.

When I was around seven years old, my dad owned an auto-body repair and restoration shop, and he spent countless hours in the garage working on cars. As a kid and even to this day, I always looked up to my dad and idolized him.

Because of my respect and admiration for my dad, I longed to be where he was. I would spend a great deal of time in the garage with him, and I am confident I drove him crazy. At that time, I didn't just want to watch, but I wanted to actively participate in the process. I wanted to be a key contributor to the shop. I would grab paint and masking tape and start working.

One winter, I even helped my dad knock all the ice off my uncle's brand-new Oldsmobile with a ball-peen hammer. I thought my dad would be so proud of me, but as you can imagine, he was not very happy at all. When I finished knocking all the ice off, the car was totaled out and completely destroyed. I am a father now, and I see this same mindset in my sons. They are right there with me, begging to help out any way they can. I know that won't last forever, so I try to include them as much as I can. (I also don't leave ball-peen hammers lying around the garage.)

If you think about this phenomenon, you have to ask what it is that drives young boys to want to be like their fathers and likewise with young girls and their mothers. This phenomenon changes as we get older. But I'm going to share a great secret with you: you have the potential to inspire others to greatness, and this can be accomplished by creating and inspiring a vision. When a team buys into a vision for greatness, everything changes. The members of that team are motivated to participate and contribute in significant ways.

You must first create a vision. A vision is a mental image of something or some state that you have created with your imagination. It has been said that every structure has two creations. The first creation is with the mind and the second is in reality.

Angie and I built a new home several years ago, and we created a blueprint (or vision) of what the home was to be before construction ever began. A vision should encompass a purpose with specific details, and it should not be too generic or vague.

I used to own a 1965 Mustang Fastback 2+2, and it was a wreck when I first bought it. It had rust everywhere, and it didn't run. The interior was ripped and torn, and it was difficult to imagine the car any other way. Angie and I were dating at the time, and she couldn't believe that I'd bought it.

But prior to purchasing that car, my dad and I had already restored several old cars, so I was able to visualize what the car could be. In my own mind, I pictured it exactly. I imagined it painted in white with blue Shelby stripes down the hood and across the top. I imagined new wheels and tires with a brand-new interior. I had a vision for what it would look like.

Several years later, we finished the car, and it looked even better than I had imagined it. In fact, Angie and I drove away in that very car on our wedding day. I'm confident she would never have imagined driving away in that car on her wedding day when I first bought it. In order to create a vision, you have to dream about what can be.

Another critical component to creating vision is having passion and conviction for your vision. It's not enough just to develop a vision, but you have to believe in that vision with every fiber of your being. Passion is so very important.

If you can't get passionate about your vision, then how in the world can you convince others to be? Passion is contagious.

If you want to determine a person's passion, just watch what he or she gets excited about. I'm very passionate about bow hunting. If you want to see me get excited and passionate, just mention bow hunting in my presence. I can talk about it for hours with great enthusiasm. I have become very close friends with other bow hunters in just minutes of meeting them for the first time. It's a common bond and passion that we share, and it excites me to no end.

That's the same kind of passion you must genuinely translate to your vision if you expect others to share in the cause. One way of accomplishing this is to involve your team in the creation of the vision. If a team member is involved and invested in the vision from the beginning, his passion for that vision is almost certain.

Once you've created a vision and are genuinely passionate about it, you must be able to clearly and concisely communicate the vision on a regular basis. Advertisers know this all too well. They might run a commercial eight to ten times before you ever notice. Constant communication is the key, and the same is true for communicating the vision of your team. You can have a great vision with unbelievable passion, but if you cannot effectively communicate that vision to your team, your vision will not be adopted, or it will be forgotten. Concise, clear, and constant communication of the vision is essential to achievement. As the people you lead begin to adopt the vision and become passionate about it, leading them will seem effortless.

If you apply the ten lessons you have learned from this chapter, I assure you that you will be well on your way to authentic leadership. You have been called to be a leader! People's lives are at stake, and you are the only one who can step into your unique position and make a difference. Go out and be the unique leader that only you can be.

CHAPTER 11

Wisdom

"By wisdom a house is built, and through understanding it is established; through knowledge its rooms are filled with rare and beautiful treasures."

PROVERBS 24:3–4, THE BIBLE (NIV)

W hen it is truly practiced, it is done with great eloquence and understanding, and yet it's difficult to grasp and define. It's a quality that we universally respect, but often can't quite put our finger on. It captures our interest and it captivates our hearts. Its results can be eternal. It saves us and points us north. We know it when we see it, but it's rare and elusive. What in the world am I talking about?

Wisdom.

I'm not referring to some mystical, mountaintop concept that is outdated and impractical. I'm referring to an approach to life that is based squarely on truth and reality. Wisdom is a concept and a way of living that creates pure fulfillment. It protects you, it guards you, and it strengthens you.

The Bible says, "Wisdom is a shelter" and "Wisdom preserves the life of its possessor" and "Wisdom makes one wise man more powerful than ten rulers in a city." It also says, "Wisdom brightens a man's face" and "Wisdom is better than weapons of war" and "Wisdom will save you from the ways of wicked men."[1]

Understanding and applying wisdom will literally change the way you think and live. Its power is beyond comprehension. The Bible says of wisdom, "For whoever finds me finds life and receives favor from the Lord. But whoever fails to find me harms himself; all who hate me love death."[2] How important is wisdom? God says it is a life-and-death matter.

The Bible goes on in great detail to make the case for the importance of wisdom. The eighth chapter of Proverbs delineates wisdom in the following way:

Choose my instruction instead of silver, knowledge rather than choice gold, for wisdom is more precious than rubies, and nothing you desire can compare with her. I, wisdom, dwell together with prudence; I possess knowledge and discretion... Counsel and sound judgment are mine; I have understanding and power. By me kings reign and rulers make laws that are just; by me princes govern... I love those who love me, and those who seek me find me. With me are riches and honor, enduring wealth and prosperity. My fruit is better than fine gold; what I yield surpasses choice silver. I walk in the way of righteousness, along the paths of justice, bestowing wealth on those who love me and making their treasuries full. The LORD brought me forth as the first of his works, before his deeds of old; I was appointed from eternity, from the beginning, before the world began. When there were no oceans, I was given birth, when there were no springs abounding with water; before the mountains were settled in place, before the hills, I was given birth, before he made the earth or its fields or any of the dust of the world. I was there when he set the heavens in place, when he marked out the horizon on the face of the deep, when he established the clouds above and fixed securely the fountains of the deep, when he gave the sea its boundary so the waters would not overstep his command, and when he marked out the foundations of the earth.[3]

How can you read that elaborate description of wisdom and not want to pursue it? Its benefits are beyond measure. The keys of real success and fulfillment are unlocked with the discovery and application of God's wisdom in your life. Wisdom is so valuable that we are told to pursue it over money. We are told to pursue it with everything we have.

DEFINING WISDOM

First, it's important to understand what wisdom is. Wisdom's foundation begins with a great respect for God, and it is the application of knowledge based on God's direction in your life. Wisdom isn't some collection of contrived techniques that we can master and then manipulate to our advantage. It isn't some high, lofty ideal or theory that has no place in reality. It isn't an accumulation of knowledge. There are many who have walked the earth with incredible intelligence and knowledge who are the exact opposite of wise! Knowledge outside of wisdom is simply information in a vacuum. It's a bunch of data with no organization.

When we think of wisdom, many things and people may come to mind. Thought and religious leaders such as Buddha, Confucius, Gandhi, and Solomon probably come to mind. Even characters from movies, like Yoda from *Star Wars*, might be mentioned as being wise or having attained wisdom. Wisdom is sometimes classified as knowledge or great understanding. Those demonstrating wisdom are usually seen as having a peaceful demeanor, introspective in thought, and consumed with meditation and focus.

Are you ready to approach wisdom? Are you ready to open your heart and mind to the idea of God's wisdom? It will not be an easy task. This chapter will only scratch the surface, but my hope is that it will light a fire in you for this incredible thing called wisdom.

You may have a limiting belief that says you can't know wisdom, that it's beyond your reach. Before we take this awesome journey, let me make it very clear that you have the opportunity to attain wisdom from God. I promise you this is true. Wisdom is not beyond your grasp. Don't take my word for it, take God's.

The Bible says, "If any of you lacks wisdom, he should ask God, who gives generously to all without finding fault, and it will be given to him." This is an amazing promise! However, the Bible does put a condition on the promise by stating, "But when he asks, he must believe and not doubt, because he who doubts is like a wave of the sea, blown and tossed by the wind."[4]

Wisdom is attainable if we ask and do not doubt. As you take on the task of acquiring wisdom, I encourage you to read the books of Proverbs and James from the Bible. These two books are an excellent beginning step forward in your quest for wisdom.

THE BEGINNING OF WISDOM

Let's start with what the Bible says is the beginning of wisdom. "The fear of the Lord is the beginning of wisdom, and knowledge of the Holy One is understanding."[5] "Fear" in this context means reverence or respect. So according to the Bible, wisdom begins with a connection to God in the form of respect.

Respect or reverence for God is an acknowledgment of two things. The first is that we are not God and the second is that God is God. I can't make it any simpler than that. You must acknowledge that God is the great Creator of all things. He spoke, and the galaxies came into existence. God created all things, including you and me. We must bow the knee before the eternal Creator of all things.

The problem that we have in the world today, and ever since Adam and Eve first sinned in the garden of Eden, is that we have become confused about who we are. We somehow think that we can be all-knowing and all-powerful. We think that we are God. If you are unwilling to acknowledge God and humble yourself before him, then forget the idea of attaining wisdom. It will never be within reach. Wisdom begins with a reverence and respect for God.

It is God who grants wisdom. He holds those keys, and it is impossible to circumvent him in the acquisition of wisdom.

How do we approach God and walk in reverence for him? The Bible starts off with the following words in Genesis 1:1 (NIV): "In the beginning God created the heavens and the earth." Then God created Adam and Eve and everything in the earth. At that time, Adam and Eve had a perfect relationship with God because there was no sin. God created Adam and Eve with free will, so they had the option to either obey or be outside of God's will by choosing to sin. Unfortunately Adam and Eve sinned, and all of mankind has been separated from God.

FINDING SALVATION

After Adam and Eve sinned, God made a provision. He sent his only son, Jesus Christ, to die on the cross as a sacrifice for our sin. If we choose to commit our lives to him and accept his free gift of salvation, then we will enter into a relationship with God. I do want to point out that although the gift of salvation is free, we still have to accept the gift. We continue to have free will, and God will not force himself on us.

If we elect to live our lives for God by accepting his Son, then we enter into relationship with him. Accepting Christ is extremely simple, but the weight of this decision is life-altering. Think of it like marriage. It's very simple to stand before a preacher and repeat the words, "I do," but marriage changes your entire life. Accepting Christ also changes your entire life, for the good.

You accept Christ by acknowledging that you are a sinner and asking him to reign in your life as Lord and Savior. The Bible says, "If you confess with your mouth, Jesus is Lord, and believe in your heart that God raised him from the dead, you will be saved. For it is with your heart that you believe and are justified, and it is with your mouth that you confess and are saved. As the scripture says, anyone who trusts in him will never be put to shame."[6]

If you have made this decision and genuinely acted on it, you are now in relationship with God, and you will be saved. A relationship with God comes before the attainment of true wisdom. You must be in relationship with God, and you must revere him as God and Creator.

Religion does not save. Being a good person and going to church does not save. You will never be good enough to fill the chasm that exists between you and

God without accepting Christ into your life. Once Christ has entered your life, and you are placing him as the authority in your life, you are in a position to begin attaining wisdom.

Once you start down the road of wisdom, your eyes will be open to the mysteries of the world. You will begin the practice of applying God's knowledge in your life. The application of God's principles is the expression of wisdom. Can you start to sense the monumental impact this practice will have on you? Think about the decisions you will make in the future as it relates to what you will do, where you will work, whom you will marry, whom you will spend time with, how you will respond to all that the world will throw at you.

If you become a parent or you are a parent now, consider the impact God's wisdom and direction will have on your children and your children's children. You will have God's power and direction guiding your steps along the exciting, yet dangerous path of life. I am extremely blessed because I grew up with a mother who loved God and demonstrated great wisdom. Every time I ever had a problem or issue I was struggling with, my mother would pull out her red leather Bible and point me to God's truths. She taught me a framework for using wisdom in my everyday life. I can't even begin to explain the impact that has had on every aspect of my life.

I encourage you to consider the important decision of accepting Christ into your life now and not later. Deciding to consider it later is deciding not to consider it at all.

Howard Rutledge, a US Air Force pilot who was shot down in Vietnam, shares an insightful perspective in his book *In the Presence of Mine Enemies*:

During those longer periods of enforced reflection it became so much easier to separate the important from the trivial, the worthwhile from the waste. For example, in the past, I usually worked or played hard on Sundays and had no time for church. For years Phyllis had encouraged me to join the family at church. She never nagged or scolded—she just kept hoping. But I was too busy, too preoccupied to spend one or two short hours a week thinking about the really important things.

Now the sights and sounds and smells of death were all around me. My hunger for spiritual food soon outdid my hunger for a steak. Now I wanted to know about that part of me that will never die. Now I wanted to talk about God and Christ and the church. But in Heartbreak [the name of the prison camp] solitary confinement, there was no pastor, no

Sunday-School teacher, no Bible, no hymnbook, no community of believers to guide and sustain me. I had completely neglected the spiritual dimension of my life. It took prison to show me how empty life is without God.[7]

I'm certain Howard Rutledge thought he had all the time in the world to consider spiritual things—and then everything changed in an instant. Consider how many people have lost their lives without ever having a second chance to consider what's really important. Please do not put it off any longer!

TACKLING THE BIG QUESTIONS WITH THE APPLICATION OF WISDOM

Once that decision is made, it's time to seek God for wisdom in every area of our lives. Let's tackle some of the burning questions that we all struggle with from time to time. Below are two areas that we will explore:

- How do I know what God's will is for my life?
- Is it possible to be ambitious and motivated for success and yet be content and satisfied with God's blessing in my life?

DISCOVERING GOD'S WILL

Let's begin with the idea of discovering God's will for our lives. This one is difficult because in most cases, God only reveals a fraction of his plan as we take each step forward. The Bible says, "Your word is a lamp to my feet and a light for my path."[8] A lamp only tends to light up the few steps in front of us.

As a hunter, I have spent many hours fumbling around in the woods in total darkness looking for a tree stand. One time I chose a stand location that was deep in the woods at a great distance from where I would be parking and walking in. I hung my stand in this location during the middle of the day with a good friend of mine, Nathan. This was a familiar area for me, but I would be accessing it from a direction that I did not know very well, and it would be in complete darkness with no flashlight. I also should point out that I would be walking through big woods with no cut path. The terrain was rolling timber with several deep ravines. If I veered off course, just slightly, I could end up walking in the woods till daylight. Nathan and I spent some time putting markers on trees every twenty steps to aid in the process. In the daylight, it seemed almost unnecessary to go to such lengths. I remember thinking it was a waste of time, but I didn't want to take any chances. It was a good thing I didn't!

The next morning, I was making my way through the woods. It was a cold, quiet morning with a heavy fog that had settled in. I avoided using a light to minimize spooking any game. About halfway in, I really struggled to find the next marker. I found myself burning precious time looking for the next marker that was only twenty steps away. At one point, I almost abandoned the idea of staying focused on the markers. I thought I could probably just figure it out by going with my gut. I was running out of time, as the sun would be peeking over the horizon in a matter of minutes, but I was a seasoned hunter at this point. I'd made that mistake before. The second you get off the path, it's like finding a needle in a haystack, even with the aid of a flashlight. So I remained disciplined. I would identify one marker, and I would not advance until I could spot the next marker up ahead. Eventually, I made it to my stand with just a few moments of darkness left as cover.

Following God's will is very similar. We are not God, and we are fumbling in the dark. He chooses to light our path, but sometimes only a step at a time. We sometimes become impatient. We start to think that we know better, and we take matters into our own hands. This is where wisdom goes out the window and folly enters the picture. I know, because I've been there many times in my life. I'm a take-charge kind of guy. If it appears that a solution is not being presented, then I will figure one out with or without God.

God doesn't work that way. He's the one in charge, and he's the one with the solution. We have to learn to rely on his guidance and direction. Experience will aid in this process. Once you have trusted a part of your life to God, and you've seen the result, you will start to rely on him more and more.

Every single time I have trusted in God's wisdom and not my own, he's proven to be trustworthy. Every single time. The more you trust in God, the more he will prove trustworthy. After a while, you'll trust without hesitation. It's just like day and night. Have you ever witnessed a time when night did not come? Have you ever known the earth to miss a rotation? I haven't. God is much more dependable than the rotation of the earth. He's the one who starting the thing spinning in the first place.

You don't wake up in the morning wondering if the earth missed a rotation. You don't turn on the news to make sure a day was not missed. Once you have a few experiences with God to reflect on, you'll start to build a level of trust that will not disappoint. Just as you trust in the world to keep spinning and trust in the idea that night will follow day, you can trust in God to lead you. But you need to start building those experiences, and it's never too late to get started.

Learning to discern God's will has been a topic of conversation among many of my friends and family over the years. I've heard questions like the following: How do I know if God wants me to take this job or keep looking? How do I know if this is the person God would have me marry? Should we buy the house for sale on the other side of town or keep looking? Should I make a career change, or has God called me to stay where I am? Is this the church God called us to, or should we be serving somewhere else? Are we ready for kids yet? Are we finished having kids? Should I start this new business? Has God called me to full-time vocational ministry? Should I eat the last piece of cake in the refrigerator? (I just threw in that last one to make sure you're paying attention.)

If we go back to the beginning of wisdom, we must first be in relationship to God. We must also be in obedience to him through reverence and respect. We are acknowledging that he is God and we are not, and we are trusting in him. We should ask for wisdom. After these things are in order, we should be in God's Word—the Bible.

Hank Hanegraaff wrote, "God's will is revealed in his word. Thus the only way to know his will is to know his word." [9] When I first heard that statement, I really didn't buy into it. I knew it was good to be in God's Word, but I didn't make the connection that God's Word reveals his specific will for my life. I now realize that it is essential for knowing his will. If you renew your mind daily by being in the Bible every day, God will transform your mind to be more in line with him. As a result, you will start to see things you never saw before.

A director at very large Fortune 500 company once opened up his private notes and goals through an internal company portal that was visible to all his employees. This was done by mistake, and he had no idea that all of the employees under his direction now had access to his personal notes, goals, and objectives. Over the course of a year, word spread quickly among his employees. In an effort to better understand his plans, they spent considerable time reviewing his objectives and goals.

As a result, his team performed well beyond expectations as compared to the other divisions in the company. Later, it was revealed that the employees had been immersing themselves in his notes and plans. The director shared this story with the entire company as an example of how the leaders of the organization should be more transparent with their plans, objectives, and thoughts.

Well, God has already done this by providing his Word to us. If you want to really know God in an intimate way, then start reading his Word. If you want to be in tune with God's objectives and you want insight into what God cares about, then immerse yourself into his Word. I recommend even putting parts of his Word to memory. I started memorizing Scripture years ago, and it has changed my life. I found myself really meditating on God's truths and principles when I had put them to memory.

Over time I have memorized complete passages of the Bible, including the book of James. It only takes a few minutes a day, but over a long period of time, memorization can have an enormous impact. Anytime I hear a speaker or pastor quote something from the book of James, I come to attention. My level of understanding and comprehension is cranking, because I have meditated on those words for so long. It's an amazing thing.

As you start to discern God's will on specific questions, you'll discover something I discovered when Angie and I were praying about having a fourth child. After our three boys, we really struggled to have another child. Angie miscarried three times, and we started to wonder if we should be finished at three children.

We continued to pray and be in God's Word, and we both felt this desire to have a fourth. We decided to adopt, and we began the process of adoption. As we got further into the process, we found out we were pregnant again. The adoption agency put us on hold. We then withdrew our application, and a few weeks later, we miscarried again.

It was a very confusing time for us. We really had no idea what God was calling us to do. Should we have four or stop at three? We weren't getting any younger, and our boys were getting older, but we kept sensing God was calling us to a fourth. But why were we having so many issues? It was extremely confusing for us.

As months turned into years, I really started to wonder why we had no direction or confirmation. Have you ever been there?

Then one day while I was reading God's Word, it became clear to me. God was allowing the process to take a long time because he wanted us to continue to trust in him, even when it seemed like we shouldn't. He sometimes allows the odds to become stacked up simply so he can demonstrate that he can do anything if we put our trust in him.

In our case, the process *was* the purpose. To say it another way, God's purpose was the process. We were called to simply trust in him, even if the answer was not clear and would not be presented for years. Are you willing to trust him like that?

In the Bible, a prophet named Elijah once confronted the nation of Israel about their disbelief in God. They were worshiping a false god called Baal. Elijah challenged them to a contest of sorts. He proposed that they prepare two altars, one to God and the other to Baal. The four hundred and fifty prophets of Baal should call on Baal to bring fire to their altar, and then Elijah, the only prophet of God at the time, would call on God to bring fire to his altar. Everyone agreed.

The prophets of Baal made their altar and called on Baal from morning till noon, but nothing happened. After that, Elijah asked for water to be poured all over the altar to God. At first glance, you have to question why Elijah would want water to be poured all over an altar he was hoping would catch fire. That's not exactly stacking the odds in your favor! Once water was poured all over the altar, Elijah called for more water a second and third time. He made sure the entire thing was completely drenched with water.[10]

Finally, he called on God. The Bible says this is what happened:

"Answer me, O LORD, answer me, so these people will know that you, O LORD, are God, and that you are turning their hearts back again." Then the fire of the LORD fell and burned up the sacrifice, the wood, the stones and the soil, and also licked up the water in the trench. When all the people saw this, they fell prostrate and cried, "The LORD—he is God! The LORD—he is God!"[11]

Now, imagine whatever situation is troubling you most right now. Think about the circumstances. Are they completely stacked against you? Is everything going wrong? Is the entire situation in a million pieces?

If that's the case right now for you, then relax for a moment. God's just pouring some water on your situation before he demonstrates his power in your life. I'm not trying to be cavalier or dismissive about your situation. You may be going through hell right now. I just want to encourage you that God is in control. Even if the altar is full of water, he can still light that thing into a blaze whenever his timing is right.

I recently met with a man who was going through a divorce. He listed every reason why he and his wife were not right for each other. They were not compatible. They should have never married in the first place. They each had different interests. The list went on and on and on.

You could say that water had been poured all over his situation. If you start to see water getting poured all over your situation, trust in God even more. Chances are good that he is getting ready to start a fire. In these situations, only God can start the fire, but he will not force it. You have to turn the situation over to him and relinquish control. A life completely yielded to God is the match on a can of gasoline. It is powerful and beyond comprehension. If you only see the water on your situation and fail to trust in God for the flame, then your fate will be the same as the prophets of Baal.

I know that every time I hold my little daughter, Brooke, in my arms, I am so thankful we continued to trust in God and his perfect timing. He never disappoints. I learn that more and more every day.

KNOWING WHEN GOD'S WILL IS CALLING
FOR ACTION OR PATIENCE

I've heard this question asked many times in the past. "How do I know if God is calling me to be patient and wait or if he is calling me to step out and take action?" Abraham from the Bible demonstrated both of these approaches in his life as he followed God.

At one point in Abraham's life, God promised him a child. This was an amazing promise because Abraham and his wife Sarah were well past childbearing years. In this circumstance, Abraham was called to wait on God and the fulfillment of his promise. Abraham and Sarah did not wait, and they devised a plan to "help God out." Many years had passed, and they just assumed that because of their age, especially Sarah's, they would have to put a plan into place.

So Sarah offered her maidservant, Hagar, to Abraham. Abraham slept with Hagar, and she became pregnant with a son. However, this was not part of God's plan.

There have been times in my life when I felt God's call on me in a particular direction, and I have assumed that God needed my help. Instead of being patient and waiting for his perfect timing, I've jumped the gun and plowed headfirst into some situation, all under the guise of following God's will. How about you? Have you ever been guilty of doing this?

Eventually Sarah became pregnant, and she delivered a baby boy named Isaac. God answered and delivered. I can understand how Abraham and Sarah thought this promise was not feasible because of their age, but God surpasses all understanding. If he created the universe and created Abraham and Sarah, then allowing her to become pregnant in her old age was child's play in comparison—right? Yes.[12]

Several years later, Abraham found himself in a situation that required him to take action. God called Abraham to take his only son, Isaac, and sacrifice him. This would be one situation where I think I would have thought to myself, "I'll wait for some more clarification." But Abraham had already learned some lessons about how God works at this point in his life, so he did not hesitate. He immediately took action to obey God. Once Abraham demonstrated his obedience, God provided another sacrifice in place of Isaac. This incredible display of faith demonstrated by Abraham allowed God to foreshadow his own sacrifice for the world by offering his Son, Jesus Christ.

In fact, Abraham was called to sacrifice Isaac in almost the same location in which Jesus died on the cross for our sins, hundreds of years later. How could Abraham have ever known what God was doing at that time? The fact is that he didn't, he just obeyed.[13]

So how do we apply this in our lives as it relates to knowing God's will? Has God called you to stay and wait, or has he called you to take action? The following principles from Scripture will provide some guidance:

- Be in God's Word on a daily basis.
- Be in prayer for God's will and ask God for wisdom.
- Share your circumstances with some fellow Christians who care about you and are willing to pray for you.
- If it seems that you are called to action, then move forward until God closes doors. In many cases, he will continue to open doors or he will slam them shut.
- If it seems you are called to wait, then plan to wait and be content and at peace with the situation.

Several years ago, Angie and I were just starting our family, and we were attending a great church. This was a solid church that taught from the Bible, filled with wonderful people. However, Angie and I did not feel like we were really fulfilled serving at this church. Without explaining all the details, we just felt that we were being called to serve somewhere else.

So we started asking some questions. Was God really calling us somewhere else? Or were we seeking change for the sake of change? Should we just wait to see if our hearts would be changed, or should we go ahead and start looking for a new church? It was a bit of a dilemma.

We were in the Word and in prayer daily about this entire situation. We also shared the circumstances with several people whom we trusted to be praying for us. After several months, I was not at peace, and I felt like we needed to do something. Now, if I were feeling this way without being in the Word or in prayer, then

I would have had no basis for taking action. I want to make sure that is very clear.

I also want to stress the importance of having unity in your marriage, if you are married, as it relates to any big decision in your life. If husband and wife are both in the Word and prayer every day, then another factor to consider in determining God's will is unity. Angie and I were both feeling called to look for another church. It would have been a different story if we were not in agreement.

Once all these things lined up, we decided to proceed with caution. God would either close the doors or open them up. We prayed about potential churches, and we made a list of churches to visit. I'll never forget when we attended the first church on our list. We were both very nervous. But after the service that Sunday morning, Angie and I both knew that this new church was where we were supposed to be. God gave us an undeniable peace about the entire situation.

In this case, we chose to take action and see if God was either opening or closing doors. We could have attended ten churches and never found what we were looking for, and we might have come to the conclusion that we should stay at the church we were currently attending. However, God did not work that way. He called us to the church that we call our church home today.

Our children are growing up in this church. The church has a private school that our children attend. Our closest friends attend this church. Angie and I have both been able to serve God in this church in unique ways that we wouldn't have been able to do at the church we were attending. I had no idea of the incredible opportunities God had planned for us. As I look back on it now, it's absolutely amazing how perfectly the circumstances lined up for us.

I will tell you that our move was not popular with everyone we knew. There were some people who disagreed with our decision, and they made it very clear to us how they felt. One thing I have learned that has served me well is this: seek only God's will, and let the rest of the chips fall where they may. You can't make everyone happy. Anytime you make a big decision in your life, there will be people who love you very much who will either agree or disagree with your decision. If you're trying to be popular and please everyone in your life, then you'll have a tough time pleasing God. I'd rather please God than people. His plans are infinitely better.

AMBITION AND CONTENTMENT

Let's now tackle the question of ambition versus contentment. In the Bible, we are called to be content with God's blessings. Paul in the New Testament says, "I am not saying this because I am in need, for I have learned to be content whatever the circumstances. I know what it is to be in need, and I know what it is to have plenty. I have learned the secret of being content in any and every situation, whether well fed or hungry, whether living in plenty or in want. I can do everything through him who gives me strength."[14]

It is clear throughout Scripture that we are called to be content with whatever God has blessed us with. There are some who live day to day with great needs and a lack of material resources, and there are others who are living in a great abundance of material wealth. There are many who fall somewhere in between. As an entrepreneur, I have gone through swings in personal income from one end of the spectrum to the other.

Our first business was financed with my own resources, which weren't much! We went from making a very solid living to making nothing in the first year. I remember thinking to myself that this was the hardest year I had ever worked in my life, and I didn't make one dollar. Once you've become accustomed to a certain level of pay, it is really difficult to take a step back. However, I did learn a great deal, and it was a valuable experience. I learned that it is easy to start placing your trust in money and things instead of God. Take the things away, and you only have God. That's a valuable exercise.

So, given that we are called to contentment, is it acceptable to be ambitious? Is it all right to strive for a raise? Is it wrong to want to build a business or take it to another level? Am I not being content in my desire to advance? Is it all right to move to a bigger house? Is it wrong to want more? What about my personal development? Am I free to learn and study and grow, or should I be content where I am? If I am being content, then am I now becoming lazy? Could I make the argument that I am living in contentment as a means of covering up laziness?

We already know that contentment is biblical, but let's make sure we have correctly defined contentment. We will do the same with ambition.

The Bible says:

- "The sluggard craves and gets nothing, but the desires of the diligent are fully satisfied."
- "A little sleep, a little slumber, a little folding of the hands to rest—and poverty will come on you like a bandit and scarcity like an armed man."
- "Go to the ant, you sluggard; consider its ways and be wise! It has no commander, no overseer or ruler, yet it stores its provisions in the summer and gathers its food at the harvest."[15]

These verses are addressing the matter of hard work and ambition. We are called to work hard and utilize the abilities God has blessed us with. In fact, we are outside of God's will when we choose laziness or elect to waste the resources God has given us.

Oliver Wendell Holmes once said, "The great tragedy in America today is not the waste of our natural resources, though that is a great tragedy, the real tragedy is the waste of our human resources."

God has given you gifts and abilities, and you are called to practice those with great diligence. At the same time, wherever you are in the process, you should be content with God's blessings. It is possible to strive for excellence while being content. In fact, contentment in the process itself is what God has called us to.

It is possible to have a goal and a desire that God has laid on your heart for something more than you have today. Perhaps you are working toward a degree of some kind. You might find yourself at the beginning of the process as a freshman. You have the ambition to work for a four-year degree, but you can also be completely content through the process and your current status.

God will give you desires. You just have to be sure those desires align with his will, or in other words, be sure you don't have a desire that goes against what his Word says is right and good. For example, you could argue that you have a desire to be divorced and that you believe God has laid it on your heart. Well, God is not going to give you a desire that goes against what his Word already states. That is why it is so important to be in the Word of God every day.

Your heart is the real factor to consider when determining whether you have stepped outside God's plan. The intent of the heart is what God really sees and judges. One of the Bible's great men prayed:

O LORD our God, as for all this abundance that we have provided for building you a temple for your Holy Name, it comes from your hand, and all of it belongs to you. I know, my God, that you test the heart and are pleased with integrity. All these things have I given willingly and with honest intent. And now I have seen with joy how willingly your people who are here have given to you. O LORD, God of our fathers Abraham, Isaac and Israel, keep this desire in the hearts of your people forever, and keep their hearts loyal to you.[16]

The way to test your heart and determine whether you have crossed the line of ambition or contentment is by asking yourself this question: do I long for this desire because it brings glory to me or because it brings glory to God? Once your focus and driving force for achievement moves away from God and toward yourself, you've stepped out of bounds.

For example, working toward a raise and promotion at your job is not a bad thing. But if you are seeking a promotion and a raise because you are longing for the status and notoriety that it will bring, you're out of bounds. If your heart longs for the money and not for God, you're out of bounds. If you seek the approval of your peers and not of God, then you are out of bounds. What is the intent of your heart? That is the question and the key.

We are called to work hard and be diligent, and we are also called to be content. Just think about this for a minute. I am called to excellence and diligence and to try my best, and I should be content with whatever the result may be. I should be content with the process. Without contentment, we will never be satisfied. There will always be something that isn't perfect. Contentment is a sense of peace in God's provision for us. Contentment is being at peace with our situation. However, it doesn't mean that we give up on desire and diligence and hard work.

Ambition based on God-given desires, coupled with contentment, provides the perfect balance. God's design is always perfect.

As you grow in wisdom, your perspective on life will change. You will start to see things from God's perspective, and you will have a peace that will transcend your circumstances. It's an amazing way to live.

THOUGHTS TO LIVE BY

The remainder of this chapter is a collection of illuminating thoughts and nuggets of wisdom to consider as you journey toward wisdom.

Illuminating Thought 1: Be Humble. Everyone loves a person who demonstrates humility, but most people are disgusted by the person of accomplishment who beats his own chest and sings his own praises. If you struggle to be humble, you are not relying on God for your significance. You are relying on yourself. That is why you feel compelled to convince everyone how great you are. The Bible says, "Who is wise and understanding among you? Let him show it by his good life, by deeds done in the humility that comes from wisdom."[17]

Think about the type of people you respect and admire. Whom are you willing to seek advice and counsel from? I'll bet those people you are thinking of now live in humility. If you choose humility as an attitude, you will find that people will be inexplicably drawn to you. Why? They will sense your confidence. You will make yourself approachable, and you will find that doors of opportunity will be opened that you never thought possible.

Illuminating Thought 2: Be Slow to Speak and Quick to Listen. A person who lacks wisdom opens his or her mouth without truly understanding the entire situation. The Bible says, "A man of knowledge uses words with restraint, and a man of understanding is even tempered. Even a fool is thought wise if he keeps silent, and discerning if he holds his tongue."[18] If you understand a situation before you speak, you never have to restate or correct yourself when new information comes in. The Bible says, "He who answers before listening—that is his folly and his shame."[19]

Illuminating Thought 3: Be Loyal and Encouraging to Family and Friends. You should never be in competition with your family and friends. Their success should be viewed as your success. There should never be a difference between the two.

I have witnessed friends who are always competing with each other instead of backing each other up. Stephen Covey talks about this as the scarcity and abundance mentalities in his book *The Seven Habits of Highly Effective People.* Covey explains that people who live with a scarcity mentality believe that if someone around them does well, then that somehow prevents everyone else from doing well. They view life as a competition where there is one winner and one loser. If you have a friend or family member who is doing well, then you might interpret it as that person winning and you losing. This is a mindset that places you in competition with those around you. The abundance mentality is the opposite: it is a mindset that believes everyone can win. In this mindset, you see those around you as teammates, and you genuinely want to see them succeed.[20]

This perspective is an important one. If you live your life with a scarcity mentality, you will rob yourself and those around you of pure joy. You will always be in competition, and you will cut yourself off from the great gifts and abilities of your family members, friends, and colleagues.

A wise person realizes his or her own weaknesses and the strengths of the people in his or her life. Be an encourager and invest yourself in those around you. How do you handle a family member or friend who is living with a scarcity mentality? As my wife likes to say, "You kill them with kindness." Encourage that person every chance you get, and use self-deprecating humor. It will take such people completely off their game. If they make a snide comment in an effort to knock you down a notch, respond with a joke about yourself. You will demonstrate enormous confidence in yourself, and you will take the gun right out of their hand. This can be difficult at first, but it gets very easy with some practice. It can actually be fun to watch their responses when you turn the entire situation upside down.

There can be great joy in celebrating in the successes of those around you. The opportunity for celebration grows exponentially when you are genuinely rooting for others in your life as compared to just rooting for yourself.

Illuminating Thought 4: Choose Your Friends Wisely, but Be Gracious to Everyone. The summer before I started my freshman year in high school, my mom and dad gave me some advice that has served me well. They told me to be friendly with every-one I came into contact with, but to be cautious with my close friendships. Throughout high school, I found myself transcending the social strata. I had friends across a wide spectrum of groups, and I've continued that philosophy throughout my life. I really enjoy the diversity of my friendships. At the same time, I am careful about entrusting close friendship to just anyone. George Wash-ington once said, "Be courteous to all, but intimate with few, and let those few be well tried before you give them your confidence."

It is common for us to want to spend time with those who are like us, but I encourage you to expand your horizons and be willing to converse with anyone, even if they are different from you. I also caution you to be wise and discerning about who you bring into the inner circle of your friendships. You want to make sure you are surrounding yourself with people who will challenge you and encourage you and be a positive influence on you. I've had to make the difficult decision in the past to end some friendships. I wasn't trying to be mean or pride-ful, but I had a couple of friends who were a negative influence on me. They were more of an influence on me than I was on them. In those situations, it is wise to keep a safe distance while still being friendly and nice.

You will become like the people you spend time with. Be wise in choosing those friendships. Don't be afraid to spend time with people more successful than you! Warren Buffett once said, "It's better to hang out with people better than you. Pick out associates whose behavior is better than yours and you'll drift in that direction." Likewise, be willing to spend time with others who may be heavily influenced by you. Just be sure that the relationships of your inner circle are pos-itive and beneficial. If they are not, you need to make some changes. The Bible says, "The righteous choose their friends carefully, but the way of the wicked leads them astray."[21]

In all your close friendships, you should be a positive influence on your friends or they should be a positive influence on you. If that is not the case, then something is wrong. Mark Twain once said, "Keep away from people who belittle your ambitions. Small people always do that, but the really great make you feel that you, too, can become great."

Illuminating Thought 5: Never Talk about Others in a Negative Way. You never know who is listening, and you never know who knows who, so keep your lips closed. If you have something bad to say about someone, say it to God. He will listen, and you won't have to worry about it getting around. If you share something with your closest friend, a person of great trust, he may share the same information with a person he trusts. Eventually everyone will know. Eleanor Roosevelt once said, "Great minds discuss ideas, average minds discuss events, small minds discuss people."

Illuminating Thought 6: Never Answer a Question of a Person Whose Intention for Asking Is in Doubt. If someone asks you a question, and you do not have a clue as to why he asked, or if the intent is questionable, then turn the tables by asking him why he is asking. The answer you get may be quite revealing! Don't ever put yourself in a position of being set up if you sense that something is out of place. The person asking the questions is the person in control of the conversation. If you're ever uncomfortable, or even just curious as to why a question has been asked, follow it up. I have sometimes even said, "I'm not going to answer that until you share with me why you want to know."

Illuminating Thought 7: Never Be Intimidated by Anyone. Eleanor Roosevelt once said, "No one can make you feel inferior without your consent." Have confidence in yourself. That confidence should be based on your relationship to God. God loves you and created you. There is no one in the world who should make you feel inferior. I don't care who they are or what they've done or what position they hold. Be who God made you to be with no regard to those in your presence.

I learned this lesson several years ago, and it opened up my world. I used to be nervous around successful people in positions of power. Once I started having confidence in myself, I no longer concerned myself with what another person thought of me. In most cases, I've received respect. In the cases where I didn't, I really didn't care anyway. This is such a liberating mindset! If you care what others think of you, you become their slave. I'm only a slave to God. Don't be afraid to be yourself.

Stephen Covey put it this way: "It is extremely ironic that the more we care about what other people think about us the less we care about people, and the less we care about what people think about us the more we begin to care for others."

Illuminating Thought 8: Be Generous. Don't ever get into the habit of hoarding things. God calls us to hold everything we have with open hands, allowing him to give and take as he sees fit. If you elect to live a life of generosity, you will experience blessings beyond comprehension. On the other hand, God also calls us to be wise in our giving. You only have a limited amount of resources, so make sure that when you give, you are giving where God is calling you to give. Giving cash to an alcoholic on a binge is probably not wise, but giving that person food is much better. Just because we are called to be generous does not mean we are called to be taken advantage of, so be wise and intentional in your giving.

Be generous with more than just your money. We are called to give of our time, talent, and treasure. God's blessings are maximized when we are obedient in our giving. I also believe that our minds are programmed to believe there is abundance when we are in a giving mode. As a result, our giving enhances our ability to handle more.

The Bible says, "Honor the LORD with your wealth, with the firstfruits of all your crops; then your barns will be filled to overflowing, and your vats will brim over with new wine."[22]

Illuminating Thought 9: Bring Solutions to the Table. Anytime you must report an issue or problem to a person who's responsible, always be prepared with a solution. Present the problem as accurately as you can, and then share that you have a possible solution. If the person who's ultimately responsible is interested in your solution, you will be asked about it. In doing this, you will always be viewed as a person who has solutions instead of the person who only brings problems.

Many years ago as an employee, I started this philosophy with my boss. As I would identify problems, I would also think to myself, "How would I handle this if I were in his shoes?" I would try my best to bring a proposed solution to the table after I presented a problem. In less than a year, my boss promoted me. He told me that I was capable of handling the team. I was demonstrating that capability every time I brought a solution to the table.

Illuminating Thought 10: Never Quit. When I first started reading books on business and real estate, I picked up a book by Donald Trump entitled *The Art of the Deal.* Trump described all the deals he had done up until the late 1980s. He referenced large, complicated projects that took enormous effort and time to pull off. He gave examples where he was turned down by banks and partners over and over again. I learned a lot about real estate and big deals by reading that book, but the one key takeaway that really stuck with me was this: "Never quit."

Once Trump decided he was going to do something, he would not stop until it was done. It didn't matter how many setbacks or how many obstacles existed. I don't believe the average person has this mindset, but you can program yourself to think in this way.

Napoleon Hill puts it this way in *Think and Grow Rich:* "Every person who wins in any undertaking must be willing to burn his ships and cut all sources of retreat. Only by so doing can one be sure of maintaining that state of mind known as a burning desire to win, essential to success."[23]

If you acknowledge that it is God who delivers and who is in control, then in what circumstances is it acceptable to quit? When is it okay for you to say, "I give up"? The answer is never.

Illuminating Thought 11: Laugh Often. Always remember that life is short. You will have plenty of time to be concerned about a whole list of things throughout your life. Just don't forget to enjoy yourself along the way. Don't ever take yourself too seriously. Remember to have fun, laugh often, and enjoy the blessings God has given you. Laughter is healthy for the soul and healthy for the body.

Humor, if it is used wisely and in appropriate circumstances, can also be a great tool for disarming a tense situation—however, great discernment must be used here. I've found that I'm the best target of my own humor. Self-deprecating humor usually puts others at ease.

Humor is a great way to bond with others. One of the things I enjoy most is laughing with Angie in the evenings about something that we've done or one of the children has done. Those are some of my best memories. I've met complete strangers, and with the mention of a particular movie or funny quote, I've had an instant connection with them. Just remember to never sacrifice someone's pride or comfort for the sake of a joke. It can sometimes be tempting, but it can also be very destructive, even if that was never your intent. Use wisdom, and remember to have fun.

Illuminating Thought 12: Be Wise with Your Money. Money is a means of daily living, and most school systems do very little to teach our children the proper use of it. The Bible talks a lot about money. Make yourself a student of finances, and learn how to be a wise steward. Your entire life will be affected by how you use your money. Below are some basics:

- Tithe on everything you make. Ten percent is a good starting point, but it should be whatever God lays on your heart.
- Always spend less than you make. If you don't, you will go broke.
- Be very careful with debt, and make every effort to be debt free. Buy cheap cars, with cash if possible. Use a modest loan to buy a house, but pay it off as soon as you can. It's far better to live in a modest house that is paid for than to live in a beautiful house with a huge mortgage.
- Buy assets that appreciate in value. Minimize purchasing assets that depreciate in value.
- Cut up all credit cards. Unsecured debt is extremely dangerous. Pay for everything with cash or a check. If you can't afford to pay for it, then don't buy it.
- Make sure you are saving for retirement and for emergencies.
- Invest in things that will make you money, not cost you money.

Illuminating Thought 13: Always Be Learning. The minute you decide to stop learning is the minute you go from advancement and growth to decline and atrophy. Program yourself to always be in a state of perpetual learning. You can learn from anyone or any situation. If you are working with someone who is difficult, then learn from the experience. You will gain the education of working with a difficult person through the greatest teacher ever, experience.

If you are talking with someone you find boring, figure out what it is that person can teach you. Every person has something that he or she is an expert in. Turn your boring situation into a learning situation. I have learned so much from just talking with people about what they do, even if it is a topic I don't know much about.

Learn to be curious about everything. Become more than just a one-dimensional person. You'll be amazed at how your life can become exciting when you learn. You should always be reading some type of book. I have a list of books, and I try to commit time each week to reading. I highly recommend reading books of varied genres and topics, and I prefer to read material that will teach me something.

Just to give you an example, I recently finished a book on the history of the US presidents. I then started a book about physics and how modern science is influencing politics in terms of nuclear war, global warming, and terrorism. After that, I read a book on value investing and financial strategies. I just started a book about eschatology and what the Bible says about the end times. My next book in the lineup is on bow hunting strategies.

I also recommend staying current with world news. It's important to be aware of what's happening in the world around you.

In every circumstance you find yourself in, ask what you can learn from it. If you take on a new challenge and fail, then get excited. Failure is a powerful way to learn. It's not a fun way, but it is powerful.

If you have a paradigm that says you can learn from any situation and experience, then you are never wasting your time if you fail. Benjamin Franklin once said, "Being ignorant is not so much a shame, as being unwilling to learn."

Illuminating Thought 14: Use Questions to Make Your Point. In a debate or discussion, you can use effective questioning to make strong points with a noncombative posture and a thought-provoking approach.

If someone makes a statement that is unsupportable, there a few ways you could respond. First, you could tell that person he or she is wrong and set off an argument that might or might not be effective. Or you could use effective questioning to put the other person in a position of defending his or her statement.

For example, someone says that the earth is not round but flat. You can respond by asking, "What research are you using to support that claim?" You've now put that person in a position of defending his unsupportable statement instead of putting yourself in a position to prove that it is wrong.

Effective questioning is also very beneficial when dialoguing with someone who is more knowledgeable than you are on a particular topic. You are positioning the conversation in a way that allows you to learn while never fully revealing your lack of knowledge.

I've also found that asking effective questions of someone you are potentially negotiating with will put that person on your side as you search for a solution together that meets everyone's needs. Asking a question like, "What could we do that would meet your needs and mine?" or "What can we do to make this happen in a way that's right for both of us?" can be extremely powerful. In many cases, a person's brain goes to work after hearing the question in order to find an answer. That person is now working with you toward an amicable solution.

Questions are extremely powerful, and it will take practice and hard work to become more proficient at effectively using them. The benefits are priceless.

Illuminating Thought 15: Seek First to Understand. Saint Francis of Assisi prayed, "Lord, grant that I may not seek so much to be understood as to understand." Have you ever been in an argument with someone and frustrated because the other person didn't understand your point of view? What about the flip side of that coin? Have you ever been guilty of not understanding someone else's position in an argument? Maybe you had a reason. Perhaps you were so confident your position was correct that it would have been a waste of time to understand the other person's point of view. Maybe you already believed you had an understanding of that person's perspective, so there was no need to address it.

In any relationship, I encourage you to make a habit of understanding the other person in every way. Even if you believe you already understand their point of view or if you believe their point of view is incorrect, take the time and energy to fully understand their perspective.

In many cases, people are willing to concede a point or change their minds if they truly believe the other person understands their point of view, even if the opposing case is not that strong. Just the feeling of being understood reduces the desire to fight. What often keeps people from changing their minds is the perception that the other person doesn't really understand.

If you take this approach to heart, you will have two potential outcomes. First, there may be something that you really didn't understand about the other person's point of view that now becomes apparent. This information, although initially overlooked, could change your entire outlook on the situation. Second, the other person will now be convinced that you do truly understand his or her position, and he or she will change to be more in line with your thinking.

Taking the time to understand the other person's perspective will take time and energy, but the process will pay big dividends in the success of the relationship.

Illuminating Thought 16: Demonstrate Confidence through Your Actions. Whenever you greet people, look them directly in the eye and give them a firm handshake. As you are shaking hands, bring your other hand around and tap them on the shoulder. This approach conveys a message of strength and confidence.

When you breathe, take deep breaths, and avoid using a shallow breath. Oxygen is extremely important to your health and well-being, so make sure your body is getting enough. If you are nervous, take slow, deep breaths to calm yourself down.

Whenever you walk, imagine that you are the CEO of a Fortune 500 company. Carry yourself with confidence and conviction. Hold your head high and use good posture. Be confident in who you are. After all, God made you to be exactly as you are.

Conclusion

You have an amazing opportunity! You have the opportunity to fulfill a place in the world that only you can fill. There is no one in the world right now who can stand in your shoes. So do you want to just get by? Do you want to come to the end and be remembered as mediocre or average? Or do you want to be great? The choice is yours completely. Your background, abilities and experience can either be your greatest asset or your greatest liability, and the difference will be based on the actions you take in the future. I believe you were destined for greatness. You would not exist today if that were not true.

In the next few days, I challenge you to start living from a solid, personal foundation. Remember that your self-worth is not based on what you do, but that it should be based on God's love for you. Embrace your uniqueness and live as an original. Quit trying to fit into everyone's mold for your life. God made you just as you are, so celebrate it and use it!

The great entrepreneurs who changed the world didn't do it by conforming to the norms of the day. Discover your own voice and don't be ashamed to use it. Live your life in boldness, and do not let fear cripple you from taking action. Establish your most important priorities and then set goals based on those priorities by focusing on the most important. Begin to see opportunity by asking the right questions and noticing the trends and big picture. Manage the risk and then take action. When you do take action, work extremely hard. Remember there is no substitute for hard work and common sense.

You have been called to lead, so start leading. Leadership does not require a position of authority. Do what is right and love those whom you lead. Rely on God as your source, and you will lead and make an impact beyond your wildest expectations.

Finally, I challenge you to seek wisdom. Wisdom begins by realizing there is a God who made you and loves you, and you are not him. Make the most important decision of your life (if you haven't already) by acknowledging God's great love for you by accepting Christ into your life.

Today is a new day. The past is the past, and you can start anew. Go out and do great things!

ENDNOTES

Quotes that are not footnoted are taken from online sources including brainyquote.com and famousquotesandauthors.com.

CHAPTER 1

1. "Abraham Lincoln," Biography.com, http://www.biography.com/people/abraham-lincoln-9382540
2. "Oprah Winfrey," Biography.com, http://www.biography.com/people/oprah-winfrey-9534419
3. "Sir Richard Branson," Biography.com, http://www.biography.com/people/richard-branson-9224520
4. "Michael Jordan," Biography.com, http://www.biography.com/people/michael-jordan-9358066
5. Theodore Roosevelt, "The Strenuous Life." Lecture, Chicago, Illinois, April 10, 1899. Read online at *Voices of Democracy: The U.S. Oratory Project,* http://voicesofdemocracy.umd.edu/roosevelt-strenuous-life-1899-speech-text
6. "Whitney Houston," WhitneyHouston.com, http://www.whitneyhouston.com/us/content/biography
7. "Whitney Houston Gets Bad Press," *Washington Post,* http://www.washingtonpost.com/wp-srv/digest/ent3.htm
8. "Steve Forbes," Biography.com, http://www.biography.com/people/steve-forbes-37588
9. "The 7 Habits of Highly Effective People Habit 2: Begin with the End in Mind," Stephen Covey.com, https://www.stephencovey.com/7habits/7habits-habit2.php
10. Mark 8:36, NIV
11. "How Much Money Is Enough?" MSN.com, http://articles.moneycentral.msn.com/Investing/StockInvestingTrading/HowMuchMoneyIsEnough.aspx

CHAPTER 2

1. Gerald Holland, "Roger Bannister: Sportsman of the Year," Sports Illustrated.CNN.com, http://sportsillustrated.cnn.com/features/ 1998/sportsman/1954/
2. Bruce Lowitt, "Bannister stuns world with 4-minute mile, *St. Petersburg Times,* http://www.sptimes.com/News/121799/Sports/Bannister_stuns_world.shtml

3. Stephen R. Covey, *The 7 Habits of Highly Effective People* (New York: Simon and Schuster, 1989), 23.

4. Proverbs 14:12, NIV

5. Covey, *The 7 Habits of Highly Effective People*, 23.

6. Ephesians 3:20, NIV

7. Jeremiah 29:11, NIV

8. Charles Colson, *The Faith: What Christians Believe, Why They Believe, and Why it Matters* (Grand Rapids: Zondervan, 2008), 36.

9. Colson, *The Faith*, 37.

10. Genesis 39:2–4, NIV.

11. Genesis 39:20–21, NIV.

12. For more reading on the life of Joseph, see Genesis 37:29–45.

13. Romans 12:2–3, NIV.

CHAPTER 3

1. John Eldredge, *Wild at Heart: Discovering the Secret of a Man's Soul* (Nashville: Thomas Nelson, 2001), 199.

2. Eldredge, *Wild at Heart,* 200–201.

3. Covey, *The 7 Habits of Highly Effective People,* 15.

4. Gordon MacDonald, *Ordering Your Private World,* rev. ed. (Nashville: Thomas Nelson, 2003), 6.

5. Ecclesiastes 2:8–11, NIV.

6. "Transcript: Tom Brady, Part 3," CBS News interview with Tom Brady on *60 Minutes* with correspondent Steve Kroft, June 2005. http://www.cbsnews.com/stories/ 2005/11/04/60minutes/main1015331.shtml

7. Galatians 1:10, NIV.

8. Psalm 139:1–16, NIV.

9. Gary W. Chapman, "All I Ever Have to Be" (New Spring Publishing (ASCAP), 1980). All Rights Reserved. Used By Permission.

10. Eldredge, *Wild at Heart,* 149.

11. "Helen Keller," Biography.com, http://www.biography.com/people/helen-keller-9361967

12. "History," Gracie Jiu-Jitsu Academy, http://gracieacademy.com/history.asp

13. Gerald Beals, "The Biography of Thomas Edison," ThomasEdison.com, http://www.thomasedison.com/biography.html

14. Rick Warren, *The Purpose-Driven Life: What on Earth Am I Here for?* (Grand Rapids: Zondervan, 2002), 17.

15. Ephesian 1:11–12, MSG.

16. Warren, *The Purpose-Driven Life*, 20.

17. Jim Collins, "Good to Great," JimCollins.com, http://www.jimcollins.com/article_topics/articles/good-to-great.html

CHAPTER 4

1. "Record Holders," Roller Coaster Database, http://www.rcdb.com/rhr.htm?m=2&t=2

2. Zig Ziglar, "Zig On… Overcoming Fear," *The Ziglar Weekly Newsletter*, http://www.ziglar.com/newsletter/?tag=job-satisfaction

3. Oswald Chambers, "The Graciousness of Uncertainty," *My Utmost for His Highest*. Utmost.org, http://utmost.org/classic/the-graciousness-of-uncertainty

4. Eldredge, *Wild at Heart*, 208–109.

5. Eldredge, *Wild at Heart*, 126.

6. Joshua 1:1–9, NIV.

7. Philippians 4:6–7, NIV.

8. Proverbs 14:32, TNIV.

9. Isaiah 9:6, NIV.

10. Max Lucado, *Fearless: Imagine Your Life Without Fear* (Nashville: Thomas Nelson, 2009), Kindle Edition, 95, Location 1124.

11. Lucado, *Fearless*, 74, Location 890.

12. "Hernan Cortes," Biography.com,http://www.biography.com/people/hern%C3%A1n-cort%C3%A9s-marquis-del-valle-de-oaxaca-39617

13. James 1:2–4, NIV.

CHAPTER 5

1. Zig Ziglar, "Why People Have No Goals Program: Part One of a Five-Part Series," *The Ziglar Weekly Newsletter*, http://www.ziglar.com/newsletter/?m=201107

2. Jim Collins, "Good to Great: Ordinary Companies, Extraordinary Results," HarperCollins.com, http://www.harpercollins.com/author/microsite/readingguide.aspx? authorID=20247&isbn13=9780066620992&displayType=bookessay

3. Warren, *The Purpose-Driven Life*, 32–33.

4. Ephesians 5:17, NIV.

5. "About Nike, Inc.," NikeInc.com, http://nikeinc.com/pages/about-nike-inc

6. "Our Starbucks Mission Statement," Starbucks.com, http://www.starbucks.com/ about-us/company-information/mission-statement

7.   "Constitution of the United States," Senate.gov, http://www.senate.gov/civics/
constitution_item/constitution.htm#preamble

8.   "The Quotable Franklin," USHistory.org, http://www.ushistory.org/
franklin/quotable

9.   "The Mission Statement that Changed the World," Stephen Covey.com,
http://www.stephencovey.com/blog/?p=14

10. Michael Jordan, *I Can't Accept Not Trying: Michael Jordan on the Pursuit of Excellence* (San Francisco: Harper San Francisco, 1996).

CHAPTER 6

1.   "Frederick W. Smith Biography," *Academy of Achievement,* http://www.achievement.org/autodoc/page/smi0bio-1

2   Romans 12:2, TNIV.

3.   "John Mayer," Wikipedia.org, http://en.wikipedia.org/wiki/John_Mayer

4.   Lieutenant Colonel Mickey Tate to Aaron L. Broyles, December 16, 2011,
via e-mail from Kabul, Afghanistan.

5.   Steven K. Scott, *Mentored by a Millionaire: Master Strategies of Super Achievers*
(Hoboken, NJ: John Wiley & Sons, 2004), Kindle Edition, Location 3298.

6.   "Thomas Edison Quotes," *Inspirational Quotes,* http://www.inspirationalquotes.me/ thomas-edison-quotes/

7.   Zig Ziglar, *Over the Top: Moving from Survival to Stability, from Stability to Success, from Success to Significance* (Nashville, Thomas Nelson, 1994), 169–170.

8.   Scott, *Mentored by a Millionaire,* Location 2990.

9.   Proverbs 3:6, NKJV.

10. Proverbs 21:30, TNIV.

CHAPTER 7

1.   Scott, *Mentored by a Millionaire,* Location 2601.

2.   "Our Heritage," Starbucks.com, http://www.starbucks.com/about-us/our-heritage

3.   "Ray Kroc," Encyclopedia.com,http://www.encyclopedia.com/topic/Ray_Kroc.
aspx

4.   "Company Profile," McDonalds.com, http://www.aboutmcdonalds.com/mcd/
investors/company_profile.html

5.   David Van Biema, "Life is Sweet for Jack Dowd as Spielberg's Hit Film Has E.T.
Lovers Picking up the (Reese's) Pieces," People.com, http://www.people.com/people/archive/article/0,,20082729,00.html

6. Luke 9:18–20, NIV.

7. Lucado, *Fearless,* 159–160, Location 1809.

CHAPTER 8

1. Matthew 14:27–28, TNIV.

2. John 14:14, TNIV.

3. Matthew 14:29, TNIV.

4. Matthew 14:30, TNIV.

5. For more reading, see Matthew 14:22–33.

CHAPTER 9

1. Proverbs 12:11, Proverbs 12:24, and Proverbs 10:4, TNIV.

2. "The Stanford Marshmallow Study," EdwardJones.com, https://www.edward-jones.com/en_US/resources/knowledge_center/money_smart_child/building_blocks/self_discipline/marshmallow/index.html

3. Proverbs 14:23, TNIV.

4. Ecclesiastes 2:10–11, NIV.

CHAPTER 10

1. John Maxwell, *Developing the Leader within You* (Nashville: Thomas Nelson, 1993), viii.

2. Proverbs 11:14, NLT.

3. Exodus 3:11, NIV.

4. Exodus 4:10, 13, NIV.

5. Exodus 3:12, NIV.

6. Maxwell, *Developing the Leader within You,* 1.

7. James 1:5, NIV.

8. 2 Chronicles 1:10, NIV.

9. Psalm 27:3, NKJV.

10. 2 Timothy 1:7, NIV.

11. Proverbs 15:22, NIV.

12. Francis Frangipane, "Protected from the Accuser," *Ministries of Francis Frangipane,* http://frangipane.org/cgi-bin/gx.cgi/AppLogic+FTContentServer? GXHC_gx_session_id_FutureTenseContentServer=4b337b600135cefe&pagename=FaithHighway/Globals/DisplayTextMessage&PROJECTPATH=10000/1000/728&sermonid=textsermon_ici264&customerTypeLabel=Weekly&sermontitle=PROTECTED%20FROM%20THE%20ACCUSER

13. Matthew 10:26, NIV.

14. Luke 19:8, NIV.

15. Psalm 25:9, NIV.

16. Matthew 23:12, NIV.

17. Dwight D. Eisenhower, "D-Day Message," *National Archives,* http://www.archives.gov/ education/lessons/d-day-message/images/failure-message.gif

18. "Lewinsky Scandal," Encyclopedia.com, http://www.encyclopedia.com/topic/Lewinsky_scandal.aspx

19. "Watergate," Encyclopedia.com, http://www.encyclopedia.com/topic/Watergate_affair. aspx

20. "Bay of Pigs Invasion," Wikipedia.org, http://en.wikipedia.org/wiki/Bay_of_Pigs_Invasion#Political_reaction

21. "Norman Schwarzkopf Biography," *Academy of Achievement,* http://www.achievement.org/autodoc/page/sch0bio-1

22. "Saint Peter," Wikipedia.org, http://en.wikipedia.org/wiki/Saint_Peter#Death

23. Hill, *Think and Grow Rich,* 139.

24. Hill, *Think and Grow Rich,* 139–140.

25. Hill, *Think and Grow Rich,* 139.

26. "Reagan Assassination Attempt," Wikipedia.org http://en.wikipedia.org/wiki/Reagan_assassination_attempt

CHAPTER 11

1. Ecclesiastes 7:12 (TNIV), Ecclesiastes 7:19, Ecclesiastes 8:1, Ecclesiastes 9:18, and Proverbs 2:12 (NIV).

2. Proverbs 8:35–36, NIV.

3. Proverbs 8:10–12, 14–29, NIV.

4. James 1:5–6, NIV.

5. Proverbs 9:10, NIV.

6. Romans 10:9–11, NIV.

7. Howard Rutledge, *In the Presence of Mine Enemies* (Old Tappan, NY: Fleming Revell, 1973), 34.

8. Psalm 119:105, TNIV.

9. Hank Hanegraaff, "5 Ways to Improve Your Life in 2009," http://hankhanegraaff.blogspot.com/2009/01/5-ways-to-improve-your-life-in-2009.html

10. For more reading, see 1 Kings 18:19–39.

11. 1 Kings 18:37–39, NIV.

12. For more reading, see Genesis 15, 16, 21.

13. For more reading, see Genesis 22.

14. Philippians 4:11–13, NIV.

15. Proverbs 13:4, Proverbs 6:10–11, and Proverbs 6:6–8, NIV.

16. 1 Chronicles 29:16–18, NIV.

17. James 3:13, NIV.

18. Proverbs 17:27–28, NIV.

19. Proverbs 18:13, NIV.

20. Covey, *The 7 Habits of Highly Effective People*, 219–220..

21. Proverbs 12:26, NIV.

22. Proverbs 3:9–10, NIV.

23. Hill, *Think and Grow Rich*, 35.